# Ahead of Time

# Ahead of Time

## *The Mystery of Precognition*

DENNIS BARDENS

ROBERT HALE · LONDON

© *Dennis Bardens 1991*
*First published in Great Britain 1991*

ISBN 0 7090 4507 7

Robert Hale Limited
Clerkenwell House
Clerkenwell Green
London EC1R 0HT

Photoset in North Wales by
Derek Doyle & Associates, Mold, Clwyd.
Printed in Great Britain by
St Edmundsbury Press, Bury St Edmunds, Suffolk,
and bound by WBC Bookbinders Ltd, Bridgend, Glamorgan.

# Contents

# List of Illustrations

*Between pages 96 and 97*

PICTURE CREDITS

Imperial War Museum: 1; Popperfoto: 4, 6, 9; P.R. Communication Ltd: 7; National Maritime Museum: 10; Michael Bentine: 12; Royal Aeronautical Society: 13, 14, 15.

# Acknowledgements

It is always impossible, in a factual and detailed work of this kind, to thank adequately and individually all who have co-operated in supplying information or facilities. Without this goodwill and help from numerous informants throughout the world, and the willingness of people to talk or write to me about their experiences, this book would have been impossible to write. I am grateful to them.

I would like to thanks Mr A.H. Wesencraft of the University of London Library, the Society for Physical Research and the Parapsychology Foundation of New York for their interest and help, and especially Granada Television for their kindness in bringing my interest in precognition to the attention of a nation-wide audience, and so bringing to my notice many interesting cases which I was able to investigate. The editor and staff of *Psychic News* have been helpful in suggesting lines of enquiry, and Christine Wiener has, with patient industry, read and checked the final manuscript.

Dennis Bardens

Savage Club
1 Whitehall Place
London SW1 2ND

# 1 Precognition – The Great Mystery

On a fine night in 1989, George Adamson, the British conservationist who had devoted most of his working life to the care and study of lions in Africa, settled down in his remote camp in Kora, north-east Kenya, hoping to cope with his ever-growing pile of correspondence.

He was not afraid of being alone. There was nothing in his life, indeed, to suggest that he had ever been afraid of anything. Even though his wife Joy, author of *Born Free* – the amazing story of their life with the lions they befriended, had been murdered by bandits in 1980, he refused to forsake his lonely, dangerous and demanding life as friend and protector of wild animals.

'My lions will protect me', he replied laconically to warnings that there were bandits around, and that tribesmen wishing to use the area for grazing their cattle resented being chased off and sent back over the border. The poachers had begun to wear military-style uniforms and to carry arms. However, at eighty-three years of age, George Adamson was amazingly fit and wiry, and a pretty sure shot himself if he needed to be.

In the gathering dusk, several lions loped along, settling near him. They made no attempt to attack. One or two knew him by sight. But they were joined by others ... and by others ... and by yet more. It was an amazing sight, one that thrilled him beyond anything. Fifteen lions in all! He had not seen so many around for months. George Adamson felt both pride and pleasure in the trust of these great beasts.

Had the lions come to protect him? Did they know, with that extraordinary gift of telepathy with which they are credited by many who have studied them closely, that the man they knew to be their friend was in danger? Did they have a premonition of coming disaster? It would not be surprising if they had – I have encountered enough examples of precognition by animals, recounted in greater detail in my recent book, *Psychic Animals* (Robert Hale, 1987).

At 1 p.m. on Sunday 22 August, George Adamson heard shots. Immediately he went into action, selecting Mohammed Maru, an employee, and three others. A few minutes earlier, Frau Inge Leidersteill, a German visitor and one of Mr Adamson's employees, had left the homestead in a pick-up truck to meet a plane at the airstrip. Adamson's party came across the truck as it was being robbed by armed dacoits. Mr Maru fled as shots shattered their windscreen, as Mr Adamson ignored warnings to slow down. His bullet-riddled body and those of his two dead employees were later found in the vehicle.

So, if the lions had come to protect him on the evening of the 19th, they could hardly have been expected to anticipate the quick-fire drama of the following day.

It is over half a century since the scientist, J.W. Dunne, wrote his sensational and trail-blazing book *An Experiment with Time*, (Faber and Faber, 1927) in which he claimed that precognition – the phenomenon by which events are seen before they happen – was a fact. Both by examples culled from his own experience and painstaking research, and by scientific argument – admittedly difficult to follow, since it included forays into the arcane labyrinths of time and space – he maintained that coming events *do* throw their shadows before, that the future can be foreseen, that there are several kinds of time and that, as a natural consequence, nothing dies.

I was on the *Sunday Express* at the time, and am glad that I went down to Broughton Castle, near Banbury in Oxfordshire, where he lived, to discuss the theories that had sent the whole scientific world agog and brought down upon his head the contumely of fellow-scientists and academics. What I wrote at that time was an accurate representation of what he was trying to say in his long thesis: this at least is guaranteed by the fact that I let him see my summary of his beliefs and assertions before I published it – as much for my comfort as his, since his arguments were as complicated as they were controversial.

Being long interested in phenomena which, for want of a better word, are broadly described as 'psychic' – (meaning happenings beyond explanation by use of our five senses – hence 'ESP' or extra-sensory perception), a few years ago I began to collect examples of precognition from many different countries. The correspondence gathered momentum and became, if I may so put it, a bit like a sorcerer's apprentice. I couldn't stop the flood, since there was not one source of information but so many. The cost of it all began to run away with me – postage, printing, the cost of processing questionnaires and following up the detail provided in them by further correspondence and, often, the provision of reply-paid slips. The expense was defrayed somewhat by a grant from the Parapsychology Foundation of New York, but I really did stick my neck out when I invited readers of the *Denver Post* to tell me what they thought would happen on a date many months ahead! It brought me, predictably, a whole lot of lunatic mail, most readers regarding it as an amusing guessing game.

The Hillsborough disaster of 15 April 1989, provides a sad and interesting example of precognition of a kind. Residents of the United Kingdom will certainly remember the broad details of that calamity, but for residents abroad I should briefly reiterate the fact of it: it was Britain's greatest sporting tragedy. What at first looked like a free fight between rival football fans was in a fact a tragedy of chaos and bad organization in and around the stadium. A total of ninety-five Liverpool supporters, mostly children and teenagers, were crushed to death when 3,000 latecomers surged into the stand.

One girl knew three weeks before the tragedy that she would die. Nineteen-year-old Sarah Hicks discussed funeral arrangements with her mother before she was crushed to death with her sister Victoria, aged fifteen.

Sarah chose the music that was played as her coffin, and that of her sister Vicky, were carried into Rayners Baptist Church – 'With or Without You' by the Irish rock group U2, and 'In an Ideal World' by The Christians. At the time that Sarah, a happy, healthy girl, discussed her funeral arrangements with her mother, the premonition was regarded as just some sort of teenage fantasy. Sadly it was not so.

Is it a sign of morbidity for young persons to foresee their own deaths? I can imagine cases of incipient mental illness where this could be so; but there are numerous instances where the people concerned were in perfect mental and physical health. One of the most poignant cases was that of 24-year-old Stephen Cummins, murdered by the IRA in March 1989. A lance-bombadier in the Royal Artillery, he was one of two soldiers killed in Northern Ireland when terrorists exploded a 400 lb land-mine beneath an Army Land-rover in Buncrana Road, Londonderry. The blast was so violent that it was heard thirty miles away.

Some time before his death, Stephen sent his parents a sealed envelope with instructions that it was to be opened only after his death. Inside was a letter thanking them for their love and care, and containing a poem which clearly indicated a presage of his own death:

> Do not stand at my grave and weep
> I am not there. I do not sleep.
> I am a thousand winds that blow
> I am the diamond glints on snow
> I am the sunlight on ripened grain
> I am the gentle autumn rain.
> When you awaken in the morning's hush
> I am the swift uplifting rush
> of quiet birds in circles flight.
> I am the soft stars that shine at night.
> Do not stand at my grave and cry
> I am not there. I did not die.

That letter was not written by someone with a morbid mind of gloomy foreboding. All soldiers know that their duties involve risk – death being one possible hazard –

especially in what has for so long been the battlefield of Northern Ireland. But Stephen, specifically, had it in mind that a valediction was necessary, and acted upon it.

In November 1988, Nigel Dempster, the *Daily Mail* columnist, revealed that Christina Onassis, the fabulously rich Greek heiress, had a premonition of an early death. She told a friend that she did not expect to live to be forty. She was right.

I little imagined that a subject which has absorbed me for so many years, and which had been researched in many parts of the world, would one day involve me personally. But so it proved.

In November 1985, my son Peter called to collect me, my wife Marie, and her niece to take us along to his new family home in Kingston, Surrey. He and his family had lived for some years in Putney, and as his mini-car was somewhat cramped compared with other vehicles, I usually had difficulty in adjusting the safety-belt on the front seat by his side. Because the journey was short, he often said, 'Oh, just drape it round you.' This isn't what one should do, but I did it.

It was a fine, sunny afternoon, with perfect driving conditions, yet unaccountably I was on this occasion concerned about the belt and, somewhat to my son's irritation, and out of character, I persisted in testing it. He was about to drive off when I said, 'Hold it. Show me how to fix this belt.' This he did, and again I stopped him. 'Show me how you disengage it.' I then managed to engage the belt myself, and again Peter was about to drive off, and again I stopped him ... 'Not yet,' I insisted, 'I want to know that *I* can disengage it too.' I then managed to undo the belt, then fix it again.

Within half an hour we were in an almighty crash which would quite certainly have cost me my life had I not been so unaccountably persistent.

The safety-belt had prevented me going through the windscreen; even though the forward thrust put tremendous pressure on my chest, with my nose about half an inch away from the windscreen, I was at least alive. There were, in fact, unwelcome, after-effects which are irrelevant to my main point, and, indeed, my wife's seemingly small wound would not heal and after months of pain she died after hospital treatment.

I have always wondered why I was so insistent about the safety-belt, for I had never bothered before. Even on this occasion, I had no foreboding or misgivings about our run-of-the-mill journey; I was not tense or apprehensive in any way, just determined that on this occasion I would not travel without being satisfied that the belt worked and was properly in place. It was not a case of precognition in the sense that I understand and use the term; precognition is knowledge of some future event, whether distant or near, and the sort of knowledge which could not be gained by normal instincts and methods of deduction. True precognition requires some knowledge of detail, the information in question being unaccountable. However, premonition and precognition appear to have some relationship; the former, perhaps, being a milder and less dramatic symptom of the latter.

The year 1989 was not to finish without yet another personal experience which gave me food for thought. My work had been dragging somewhat; like many people, I had reached the point where I needed a change of scene and air. I wasn't ill, but a bit tired from long hours and unremitting work.

A friend of mine, who is both a doctor and a surgeon – Dr Lee Minton, President of the Minton Foundation (USA) – and has homes in London, South Carolina and Tennessee, suggested that I should take the top floor of his seashore home on Pawleys Island, South Carolina. 'It's quiet and peaceful. You could concentrate well. It's self-contained with its own bedroom, living-room, verandah, kitchen and bathroom. It faces the Atlantic, only a few yards from the ocean itself. You'd love it.' He was going away on an archaeological dig in Italy, and by way of encouraging me to take him up on his generous offer, sent a travel credit through a travel agency.

What could be simpler? All I needed to do was to get to Heathrow Airport. Everything would follow on from there … but I didn't go.

'But why not?' said Dr Minton.

'I want to concentrate on my work here.'

'I'd have thought it would be easier to concentrate here, but the decision is yours.' He sounded disappointed, if not a little puzzled. I had no ties to keep me in London. I love travel and am usually looking for an excuse to indulge in it. In this instance everything was laid on, and it wouldn't have cost me a penny. As courteously as I could, I stuck to my refusal. Like my insistence on my son showing me how to fix and unfix the safety-belt in the car shortly before a near-fatal crash, some inner instinct made me act out of character.

Once again, it proved fortunate that it did. At the time I would have been in that house in Pawleys Island it turned out to be far from peaceful. As Dr Minton told me in a brief letter:

> ...we have experienced the worst hurricane of the century. South Carolina is a virtual war zone. Our island was hit hard, being relatively near the eye of the storm.
>
> Of good fortune was the fact that my home was in the island's centre and the damage was less there.
>
> I lost the upper porch, roofs of my living room and dining room, with great heaps of rubble under the house. All garden, trees, vegetation and planting gone ... the dune which has taken 35 years to build up ... there is no trace except a great heap of sand behind my house ...

However, if there was any element of precognition in my handling of this invitation, it was at least on a subliminal, and certainly not a conscious, level. My decision was not actuated by fears or foreboding of any kind. Nevertheless, out of character, having regard to my normal love of travel, I didn't go and thereby missed the fury of Hurricane Hugo.

One morning in February 1975, a crowded London underground train failed to stop at the Moorgate platform and ploughed into a dead-end tunnel, killing forty-four people and injuring many more.

Among those who escaped were four passengers who had used the line for years and set themselves in the front

– that is, the *first* – carriage. Because of a last-minute premonition, on this particular day all chose the *fourth* carriage. Of those killed, most were in the tangled and telescoped first and second carriages.

It was a similar instinct or hunch which, in October 1967, prompted Mrs Helen Peters of New Jersey, USA, to rush to the telephone, get through to the New York office of British European Airways and tell them of her overpowering conviction that the plane in which her husband was travelling was about to crash. The staff at BEA were puzzled and sympathetic, assuring her that all was well. Shortly afterwards the BEA Comet crashed in the Mediterranean off the coast of Cyprus, killing all sixty-six passengers and crew.

What prompted Mrs Peters to wake, sobbing and distraught, and to take the action she did? The absolute conviction that she was right, that she had received information by means she could not explain. She knew of something before it happened.

Why, during the fiercest days of the Blitz on London, did that old war-horse Winston Churchill, so indifferent to the hazards of battle and oblivious of the gunfire and falling bombs, enter his car during the blackout by a totally different door, instead of getting in his usual seat? The unaccustomed choice saved his life. A bomb exploded, his car was lifted, veering crazily on two wheels, and narrowly missed overturning. Discussing with his wife why he had chosen the opposite side of the car, although the door was being held open for him on the usual side, he remarked, 'Something said "Stop!" before I reached the door held open for me. It then appeared to me that I was told I was meant to open the door on the other side and get in and sit there – and I did.'

One may ask too how President Lincoln *knew* he would die by an assassin's bullet. For him it was not a premonition, but a case of certainty. Weeks before his death he described how, in a vivid dream, he had left his bed and wandered downstairs. As he wrote:

There were no living persons in sight, but the same

mournful sounds of distress met me as I passed along – I kept on until I arrived at the East Room, which I entered. There I met a sickening surprise. Before me was a catafalque on which rested a corpse wrapped in funeral vestments. Around it were stationed soldiers who were acting as guards; and there was a throng of people, some gazing upon the corpse, whose face was covered, others weeping pitifully. 'Who is dead at the White House?' I demanded of one of the soldiers. 'The President', came the answer, 'he was killed by an assassin.' Then came a burst of grief from the crowd, which awoke me from my dream.

On 14 April 1865, five days after the surrender at Appomattox, Lincoln was killed by an assassin's bullet at Ford's Theatre, Washington, DC. Three-and-a-half hours before his death he told his guard, William E. Crook, 'Crook, do you know, I believe there are men who want to take my life, and I have no doubt they will do it.' When the President left he did not say, as was his usual custom, 'Goodnight, Crook,' but '*Goodbye*, Crook.' That was at 7 p.m. By 10.30 p.m. he was dead.

Spencer Perceval, British Prime Minster (1762-1812) had a similar prevision of his violent death. It happened on 11 May 1812 when John Bellingham, a merchant who attributed his bankruptcy to the Tory measures for which, both as Chancellor of the Exchequer and First Lord of the Treasury, and when he became Prime Minister in 1809, he had been responsible, shot him in the House of Commons lobby.

For over a week, Perceval had a strong premonition that he would be killed soon, even though he knew of no enemies who could contemplate such a thing; he told his wife of his conviction, and put his affairs in order should it come to pass. Strangely, on 3 May 1812, the manager of some mining concerns in Cornwall, John Williams, had a persistent dream – it occurred three times in a night – of a man in a snuff-coloured coat with metal buttons, shooting a man 'dressed in a blue coat and white waistcoat.' The first man produced a pistol and shot the other. As he fell dead, the dreamer just knew that it was the British Prime Minister. He told his wife, who dismissed the dream as a nightmare, and even told friends that he intended to travel to London and warn Perceval. He was dissuaded from doing so, it being in the highest degree unlikely, it was said, that the eminent man would see him. On the day before his murder, Perceval told his friend the Earl of Harrowby that he had dreamed of being assassinated. The Earl tried in vain to persuade him to stay away from the House of Commons that day.

The Aberfan landslide in 1966 shook the British nation, making the little village in South Wales the centre of attention both in Parliament and the press. Once Aberfan had played its proud part in the Welsh mining industry; now the colliery was closed but nothing had been done to make the disused workings safe. The tip loomed dark overhead, and pessimists predicted that it threatened the community. Many had scientific knowledge to shore up their warnings, to which the National Coal Board, as a subsequent Tribunal of Enquiry found, proved stupidly and callously indifferent – indeed, even *after* the tragedy the Board refused to take any positive action on moving the remaining tips until the Aberfan people formed a Tip Removal Committee.

A friend and fellow-member of the Society for Psychical Research – Dr J.C. Barker, a member of the Royal College of Physicians and a distinguished psychiatrist (to the Shrewsbury Group Hospital Management Committee), was, like myself, keenly interested in the phenomenon of precognition. He wondered whether so great a disaster had cast its shadow before; had anyone foreseen it?

He visited Aberfan, and made known his wish to be contacted by anybody who could prove that they had foreseen the tragedy to a degree of detail greater than mere foreboding or premonition.

The response was as startling as it was disturbing. Within weeks, he received seventy replies from people who claimed to have foreseen the disaster or fragments of it. One of the most tragic and extraordinary accounts he came across concerned nine-year-old Eryl Mai who remarked to her mother over breakfast weeks before the disaster: 'Mummy, I'm not afraid to die.' There had been no preamble to this observation. She told her mother, in response to her shocked questioning as to what the remark meant, that she had had a vivid dream in which everything went black, and she and her friends died. She described it in a matter-of-fact way, not from any childish desire to draw attention to herself by saying something deliberately absurd. For whatever reasons, her mind was ahead of time.

*Ahead of Time* – yes, of time as we conceive it. But I believe we do this incorrectly, basing our explanations and theories upon false premises. We assume that time is a true dimension, running like a railway track, singly and straight ahead, the moving train being the present. Sir James Jeans, the former Astronomer Royal, alerted the scientific world as early as November 1930, to the falsity of this assumption, in his Rede Lecture to the University of Cambridge:

> The fundamental laws of nature, in so far as we are at present acquainted with them, give no reason why time should flow steadily on: they are equally prepared to consider the possibility of time standing still or flowing backwards. The steady onward flow of time, which is the essence of the cause-effect relation, is something which we superpose [sic] on to the ascertained laws of nature out of our own experience; whether or not it is inherent in the nature of time, we simply do not know.

Putting it another way, we think of time as a distance between two points, along which something we choose to call the present moves in one direction only. So far as we are concerned, our conception of time begins at birth and ends at death, although most of us accept that it probably continues after we die. This would constitute a single dimension, namely, length. Two other dimensions which give substance and shape to things are breadth and height. But Einstein, with his quantum theory, linked time with space. Proofs of the validity of his theory of relativity have since been discovered, although the revelation that other galaxies are moving away from ours, and that the universe is expanding could still produce surprises.

That our conception of time has been an abstraction – illusion, if you like – was revealed, however, long before Einstein postulated his more specific theory. As early as the eighteenth century the French philosopher, Etienne Bonnet de Condillac, (1715-1780) declared:

> You apply your own duration to everything outside you and by this means you imagine a common measurement, instant for instant, with the duration of everything in existence. Are you not thereby realizing an abstraction?

About two hundred years later, we find Sir James Jeans endorsing Condillac's view, explaining our mistaken attitude to time in a vivid analogy which can scarcely be better:

> When we weld together length and breadth we get an area – let us say a cricket field. The different players divide it up into its two dimensions in different ways; the direction which is 'forwards' for the bowler is 'backwards' for the batsman and is left-to-right for the umpire. But the cricket ball knows nothing of these distinctions: it goes where it is hit, directed only by the laws of nature which treat the area of the cricket field as an indivisible whole, length and breadth being welded into a single un-differentiated unit.

But, says Jeans, supposing one welds such an *area*, say a cricket field, which has two dimensions, with *height*, one has a space of three dimensions. We are accustomed to gravity and for us 'height' means that direction in which it is hardest to throw a cricket ball a given distance. But out in space our ideas of horizontal, vertical disappear and have no meaning; nor has 'height' – where is the 'floor' or base from which to judge it?

However, Einstein's theory of relativity is based on the assumption that these three dimensions do not constitute space, which is four-dimensional; the three dimensions are joined to the dimension of time. This conception takes us right away from our railway-track idea of time and compels us to look at one of the most complex and baffling problems of all, and one with which, within my own manifest limitations, I propose to deal: precognition.

What is precognition?

Briefly, foreknowledge. Precognition is awareness, however reached, of fact and circumstances which cannot be accounted for by science or logic. Anything that can be explained in terms of subconscious knowledge, or by interpreting a known past sequence of events, or by an intelligent assessment of the situation based upon detailed information, cannot rank as precognition. The weather forecaster, the financial adviser, the political commentator and the army general are not being precognitive when they tell us, respectively, that we are in for a rainy summer, that the pound or dollar will drop in value, that there may be brushes on the Sino-Russian border, or that an anti-tank weapon will not prevail against a new and more formidable tank. They rely upon expert and empirical knowledge.

Of all psychic phenomena, precognition is both the most puzzling and the most disturbing. Even to acknowledge that it is possble makes us uneasy and implies a conflict. How can something be seen before it happens? Our senses respond to events and stimuli as they happen; our perception is the effect, what we perceive is the cause. How can it happen in reverse? Does the future exist already, neatly plotted before us and, if it does, what of our free will and individuality? Many feel already that death is a cruel and futile end to a lifetime of stress, endeavour and adaptation – are we to be denied even the consolation that we can to some extent shape events between birth and death? What is the point of decisions if everything is predetermined? It is the process of adaptation, of meeting challenges and overcoming difficulties that gives life half its zest and purpose. In brief, how can the effect precede the cause?

Next, you may say: what about the prediction business? I am not concerned with that diffuse and profitable world of soothsayers, who range from tarot card readers to sand diviners, from society clairvoyants to newspaper astrologers. A very great number of them have enormous followings, and I do not doubt that some proportion of their predictions prove correct. In some senses it is a happier world than the world of precognition, since few people want to pay for being made to feel miserable, and a higher proportion of paid forecasts are on a happier note than is the case with prevision. If professional seers are excluded from this book, it implies no assessment of their merits or demerits. Nor is it primarily an examination of the world of dreams, although dreams do necessarily come into it. Dreams, we know, are on a different level of consciousness, and sensitive electronic instruments have enabled us to measure, to a degree hitherto impossible, the different levels. Until recently it has been fashionable to talk of *the* subconscious mind. Hypnotism has long proved that it certainly exists and contains an immense fund of surprising and often 'forgotten' knowledge; but the assumption that one term comprises all these levels is unwarranted.

Cases of precognition have been reported for centuries. There are some odd curiosities. The first Marquess of Dufferin and Ava (1826-1902), British diplomat and administrator, while staying in Ireland, reported seeing a vision of an ugly and terrifying man carrying a coffin. Hallucination or not, that is what *he* saw. Later, when he was British Ambassador in Paris, he was waiting for the hotel elevator with a gathering of people. When the elevator descended and the doors opened, and people made way for him to enter first, he drew back in horror, and refused to enter. *He recognized the operator as the repulsive phantom he had seen.* The others crowded into the lift, which began its ascent. The cable broke, and the elevator with its screaming occupants crashed down the shaft, killing them all.

It is often said that previsions are usually of unpleasant or unhappy things. This would appear so, but there are no statistics by which one could form any estimate. There is, however, one outstanding example of a prevision which gave somebody satisfaction: on 23 February 1885, a murderer, John Lee, was led to his execution. On the scaffold he stood upon the double trapdoor, whose two parts, hinged and opening downwards, would ensure his drop when the bolt were withdrawn. To make certain that the pressure was even, a prisoner had to stand with a foot on each door.

On the night before his execution, Lee had had a strange dream. 'I was led through the reception out to the hanging place,' he told the warders the next morning, 'but when they placed me on the drop they could not hang me, for there was something wrong with the machinery of the drop. Then they took me off from the drop and took me (instead of the way I had come) around the A wing and back through the A ward to my cell.'

The warders related his story to the prison governor, as a result of which rigorous checks were made beforehand to ensure that the mechanism was working. However at the execution the drop refused to work, despite several attempts to make it do so, and notwithstanding the numerous proofs of its effectiveness beforehand.

True to the prisoner's prevision, they gave up the attempt to hang him and led him back to his cell by the route he had foretold. Needless to say, in those tough times, he had not the least personal expectation that his dream would come true. Not until the chaplain visited him in his cell and informed him that his sentence had been commuted to penal servitude for life, did he count himself (by comparison) fortunate. The story is related in Lord Halifax's *Ghost Book* and was attested by the chaplain of Exeter Prison, the Reverend John Pitkin, two warders, and the prison governor.

A curious hint of precognition is implied in an unexplained happening on the morning of 7 December 1939, when in front of the primary school in Owensville, Indiana, USA, were written the words, in huge letters: 'REMEMBER PEARL HARBOR'. Everyone at the time was puzzled by its meaning. But the message was certainly remembered at the time of the Japanese attack on 7 December 1941, when a large Japanese naval force including six carriers, under Vice-Admiral Nagumo, struck at the US Fleet lying in Pearl Harbor. Over 300 aircraft took part in the attack, which caught the American defences completely by surprise. To this day, nobody knows who wrote that strange message two years earlier, or why.

My own researches into the phenomenon of precognition have, over the years, involved much effort and no little expense, for investigations so often produced material out of all proportion to the trouble involved.

I extended this experiment to many other countries. One correspondent in Singapore sent me lengthy letters in Chinese characters, which of course I could not read, but, feeling that it was unfair and uncivil to invite correspondence and then neglect it, I paid a Chinese student at London University to translate it. When I did so, I had the surprise of my life, for all his letters were written *before* the American landing on the moon, and they predicted, strangely and accurately, that they would find 'glass marbles!' Well, as we all know now, the space explorers did bring back tiny little balls of glass. A diplomat whom I asked to visit this correspondent in Singapore reported back to me that he was a young student who knew not a word of English and even less about science. A strange business.

An appearance on Granada Television in Mike Scott's series *The Mysteries* was productive of some very interesting material, since the station, very generously, not only enabled me to explain the purpose of my research and the nature of the phenomena, but put my name and address up on the screen for viewers to copy.

It should not be assumed, of course, that information vouchsafed to me is accepted at face value. Obviously, I have no wish to play the part of inquisitor or to impugn the good faith of people who have experienced spontaneous phenomena to which there were no witnesses, but it is reasonable to check facts when there are facts to be checked, and to cross-check with corroborators where these exist, where this can be done without detriment to the feelings or the livings of those concerned. I am very grateful to the numerous correspondents throughout the world who have co-operated with me in my fascinating quest.

Clearly, precognition cannot be explored without upsetting many preconceived or established ideas. Obviously, if precognition, which is knowledge of the future, is a fact, our ideas of time need revision. The late J.W. Dunne set the trail with the publication of *An Experiment with Time* in the thirties. I had long discussions with him on my visit to Broughton Castle, where he studied in the enveloping silence of a room whose walls were ten feet thick. Lucid, modest, fresh-complexioned and youthful, this scientist made us rethink our notions about time, and came nearer to proving immortality by scientific means than anybody before or since.

For readers unfamiliar with Dunne's theories, I strongly commend a perusal of his works. He was a man of supremely practical turn of mind, designer of the first British military aircraft, a mathematician and a philosopher. He began recording his dreams, to discover that they gave inexplicable glimpses of the future. This convinced him that time was not the simple measurement we had imagined, a dimension along which something called 'the present' moves forward from one end to the other. Precognition raises some important questions. *Would it be any advantage if we did fully understand precisely how and why it occurs, to the point where we could see into the future at will?* Might it not break the pluck of some people if they could see the trials and deprivations, the accidents, heartaches and bereavements that lie ahead? *Is precognition a capacity, or a spontaneous phenomenon?* Do environmental factors predispose people to it, and do genetics play a part, some people being more able to foresee the future than others? The answers to these questions may be found in due course. For the moment, let us consider some cases of people who found themselves ahead of time.

# 2 The Boy Who Knew

The point of my call at a small terrace house – one of several in a row – in the typically English county town of Aylesbury in Buckinghamshire was to find out more about the death of a little boy who had foretold his fate. Paul had lived there happily with his family but for no reason anyone has been able to explain, had told his father that he would die when he was eight years old – and he did.

No disability, no anxiety over his health (then perfect), nothing morbid overheard, could account for his inexplicable conviction.

Mrs Stan Czarnecki showed me into a cheerful front parlour. She was, of course, expecting me – I had explained my interest in precognition; she was perfectly willing to talk about the family tragedy. I had explained how important corroboration was in such cases. She understood. I noticed that a cabinet containing pieces of favourite china and souvenirs had, on top of it, several photographs of a merry and intelligent-looking little boy.

'Is that Paul?' I asked.

'Yes. That's Paul. Sonia took it.'

Sonia, the dead boys's sister joins us. She is pretty and self-assured. She was a constant companion to her younger brother and misses him very much.

Another brother, seventeen-year-old Michael joins us, then the head of the family, Stan Czarnecki, a former Pole who, after the invasion of his country during the short-lived pact between Nazi Germany and the Soviet Union, fought in Africa, Iraq and Italy with the British Eighth Army. Of those distant dramas – the invasion of his homeland, the massacres, concentration camps and battles – he never speaks. But the Czarneckis are a close-knit Catholic family, and of Paul, the missing member, there is almost daily mention.

In every corner of the home there are reminders of the boy who foresaw the future. There is a giant toy Panda, photographs of Paul at school, at play and, towards the end of his life, in a wheelchair. Pride of place is taken by a coffee-pot which he bought from his post-office savings.

A lean, silky black cat enters the room. It jumps up on to the window-sill and stares into the small cul-de-sac street ... Often it would go up to Paul's old room to look for him there.

'She won't believe that Paul's gone', Mrs Czarnecki explains. 'None of us can really believe it either. He seems still with us.'

'I dream of him every night', Sonia interposes. She was deeply attached to her younger brother. The Czarneckis are, indeed, a close-knit family.

I come to the point of my visit.

'Tell me,' I ask Mr Czarnecki, 'how Paul predicted his own death.'

'We don't want for anything,' he explains, 'but we're careful with money; I've always taught the children to save for the things they'll really need – give them the most pleasure. Paul, like his brother and sister, had a post-office savings account in Aylesbury. He'd stamp a card until it was worth £5, and then we'd go together to the Post Office to pay it in.

'I took him to the Post Office to pay it in, and he said to me suddenly, "Why are you taking me to save my money? I won't need it for long. I'll die when I'm eight".'

'When was this?'

'In 1971. He was six years old then.'

'Had he any reason you can think of to say such a thing? It seems an extraordinary remark from so young a child – or any child, for that matter.'

'No reason at all. He was perfectly fit and perfectly happy. He was companionable, at ease with family and friends, interested in everything, merry and playful.'

'Had he been hearing about death or illness? Was there

any reason why his thoughts should have been on death?'
'None whatsoever.'
'What was your reaction?'
'Puzzled, of course. And disturbed. It seems such a strange and unexpected thing to say.'

Mr Czarnecki could not forget that remark, but never reverted to it. Nor did he mention it to his wife, for fear of upsetting her. Therefore she did not see the coincidence of another incident that happened later.

On returning to England (the Czarneckis married thirty-five years ago), Mr Czarnecki set up home in Wendover, near the Royal Air Force camp at Halton, where he worked. Mrs Czarnecki puts human relationships before possessions – she is a miner's daughter from Wales – but is nevertheless a conscientious housewife who likes to improve the home as finances permit. There was just one coveted luxury she was saving up for – a silver coffee-pot. Not something they would expect to use very often, but nice to bring out on special occasions, and very handsome anyway in a glass-fronted cabinet.

One day Paul said to her, 'Mummy, why don't you draw my money out? I'll never need it.'

'Of course you will,' his mother replied. 'Of course you'll need your savings. That's for when you grow up and get married.'

'I'll never get married,' Paul replied, as though the fact was unarguable. Mrs Czarnecki thought it a strange reply.

Although Mr Czarnecki wondered to himself if anything would happen, he had never let Paul think that he had ever taken his remark seriously. Indeed, when Paul had declared categorically that he would die when he was eight years old, he had said, 'Of course you're going to live long', and dismissed the subject.

As time went on there was nothing to feed any misgivings which his remarks to his father and mother could have aroused. Paul was perfectly fit, mentally and physically. He mixed easily in the infants' school, where he was popular with teachers and pupils. He loved playing football, liked drawing, making montages of paper shapes, listening to the radio or watching television. Later, at Elmhurst Middle School, in Aylesbury, it was the same story. He had as much mischief as one would expect, even hope for, in an normal boy, but was well behaved, liked his lessons and got on with everybody. He was especially brilliant at mathematics.

Not until March 1974, did Paul's precognition show signs of coming to pass. His parents, his teenage brother Michael, his sister Sonia, began to notice something amiss. Once, when he was undoing sweet-wrappers, his hands and arms went completely cold. On another occasion, when Sonia took him to the local discothèque and he was stomping around happily to the music, he seemed unable to stand properly. On the way home with his sister and friends, he fell around uncertainly, as a drunk might, and nobody could be sure whether he was having a joke or under a true disability, for he was laughing with it.

The local doctor could find nothing wrong with him. Even so, Mrs Czarnecki was certain by now that something *was* drastically amiss. She took Paul to Stoke Mandeville Hospital near Aylesbury, on the second day of May 1974, when Paul was still eight years old. Dr Michael Salmon, the consultant paediatrician, suggested that the boy should return the following day for brain X-rays. This was done, and at noon that day Dr Salmon broke the news to her: 'Paul has a blood clot. I'm arranging transport for him to go straight away to Radcliffe Hospital, Oxford.'

At Oxford doctors and specialists investigated his condition. An operation was deemed necessary, and fixed provisionally for the following day, Saturday 4 May. When it was realized that this would be Paul's ninth birthday, it was postponed so that he could enjoy his presents and cards.

The operation failed – now Paul could neither walk nor talk. He was transferred to the Churchill Hospital in Cowley, where Mrs Czarnecki was told that nothing further could be done. Paul, she was told, would die within twelve months. When she had recovered from the shock of the news, Mrs Czarnecki knew what she must do.

'In that case,' she said, 'I will take him home with me.'
Being herself an experienced nurse, she knew she could
give him all the continuing care his condition would
require, while as his mother she was determined that he
should, until the end, be in the midst of his family and
friends.

Now began the careful, loving, yet heartbreaking plan
to ensure that Paul's last days should be made as happy as
possible. Everyone behaved normally, as though oblivious
of the impending tragedy. But it was far from easy. One
day before Paul had lost his speech, Sonia, who was
deeply devoted to her brother, had the greatest difficulty
in concealing her distress when Paul suddenly said to her,
'Kiss me. I'm going to die. I feel I've got some disease that
is destroying me.' Then it had been almost more than she
could bear. Now it *had* to be borne. The inevitable made
them brave for his sake.

Paul's condition deteriorated rapidly. He was certainly
brave, too. Although unable to speak, and confined to a
wheelchair, physically completely helpless, he smiled
readily. He managed to convey to his family and friends
the pleasure their nearness and companionship gave to
him.

A kindly neighbour gave Paul a cat, Stinker. The two
became inseparable companions; Stinker would sleep
nowhere except with Paul. Mrs Czarnecki bought a
sunshade to fix to Paul's chair, so that he could sit
shielded from the sun in the garden. Always very fond of
flowers, Paul admired especially a cluster of mauve asters.
He would fondle them with his fingers, and once even
talked to them. Mrs Czarnecki believed that those he
touched in his declining days grew taller – considerably
taller – than the rest.

Mrs Czarnecki saw to it that he did not lose touch with
his fellow-pupils and playmates. They were fond of him
irrespective of his illness. They looked in to see him, or she
would take him to his class at Elmhurst School, and all his
classmates would gather round him and talk to him. His
condition deteriorated rapidly. At last he went completely
blind, and the pictures show him looking like a pensive

elf, smiling still yet very, very frail. Before his school broke up for the summer holidays, Mrs Czarnecki took him to his old class, and both masters and pupils talked and joked with him. A treasured memento is a last message from them, 'We hope you are feeling as well as you can be, and are keeping cheerful' signed by masters and pupils of class 14 and class 12.

Three weeks later Paul was dead. His illness that proved fatal had struck him just *before* his ninth birthday, so that his prediction that he would die when he was eight was almost uncannily accurate.

What gave this young boy, then merely six years old, this foresight? Why did he speak with such conviction, since he loved life and was not of a morbid frame of mind?

In its prescience, Paul's prophecy bears a close resemblance to the one by Eryl Mai, the little girl from Aberfan. Eryl was also emphatic that she was going to die – in a dream she had seen the school enveloped in a black cloud. And Eryl *did* die, along with 127 other children when the slag heap slid down the mountainside on to the Pantglass Junior School. How did *she* know? How did Paul know?

# 3   The Seer

Mrs Valerie Goodsell is a freelance designer, in her early thirties at the time I interviewed her, and married to an artist. She herself volunteered her age, which one would not otherwise guess, as she looks much younger. I had gone to see her because, she had informed me, she had experienced precognition several times. Her letters and statements suggested a logical mind, a care for facts, and an interest in the phenomenon of foreknowledge.

At the time of our interview, their home was at Orpington, in Kent, although they have since moved to another home in Cornwall. She emerged from a battered Land-rover to meet me at the station and impressed me at once with her self-confidence and cheerful practicality. In dealing with weird phenomena which tax credulity, it is always reassuring to find that informants have their feet on the ground; the character and personality of informants is an important factor in assessing evidence.

Soon we were sitting by a blazing log fire in a handsome studio-type lounge. Valerie Goodsell is herself artistic: it was she who had made the two huge terracotta candlesticks of a king and queen, styled in playing-card pattern. There were other touches of artistic imagination – a large faun's head in coloured glaze, hollowed at the top to accommodate a plant, as well as a lavish display of dried grasses and flowers. Mrs Goodsell also writes stories about witches and fairies. She is very frank about herself. Clearly she has seen life as an adventure and not something with carefully slotted tracks that must be followed – an open-minded approach that must have helped her in coming to terms with physical experiences.

As she put it to me in an early letter:

> I draw, I paint, I potter, I photograph, I write. I worked as a
> secretary (I was not a good one). I have worked as a
> photographic model for advertisements in magazines and
> on television. I have worked in boutiques and shoe shops.
> At present I have a stall in a market, selling wares I make
> myself, which include hobby-horses, paper flowers, mice
> and crocodiles, rag dolls and long woollen scarves. I've
> hung pictures on railings ... I write poetry and cry over
> cobwebs. I come to life in thunderstorms and reach out to
> the clouds lit up by lightning and wish I could fly ...

It will be obvious from all this that she is a person of highly
developed sensibilities. But since we are concerned with
her psychic experiences, I must establish right away that
in my considered opinion those sensibilities are under
disciplined control. She has imagination, but not to the
extent, in my view, as to render her testimony suspect or
make her liable to hallucinations. In any case, the
examples of precognition which she recounts are
corroborated. It isn't a question of what she envisaged or
dreamed about; such information as she received, and
which later was confirmed by events, she recounted to
others *before the event*. That is an important requirement in
true precognition.

Valerie Goodsell dreams a good deal, and in fair detail:

> I dream avidly and in beautiful colour. I see the most
> wonderful clothes, which would take years to make. One
> was covered [an evening dress] in minuscule feathers of
> pastel hues, each embroidered in a patter with tiny, tiny
> beads that blended with the feathers.

Long before Mrs Goodsell had even heard of J.W. Dunne,
who revealed that dreams could (and in his case did) have
a precognitive content, she made a habit of recording her
dreams. Some of these, she found, foretold the future. I
am aware of the argument which says that because
millions of people dream every night, some of those
dreams must, by some unstated 'law of averages' come
true. I agree that some might be coincidental, but when a

dream foreshadows a future event in more than one detail, the mathematical odds against such a degree of detail are very high indeed.

Let us consider a dream which Mrs Goodsell had between Sunday night and Monday morning, 25 November 1968:

> I dreamt I went into a smallish stone-type country cottage, old and old-fashioned – that is, no 'mod-cons'. It had a central path to the door. I don't think there were other houses around. There were a lot of other children (girls, I think) inside, drawing at desks or tables. Two men walked in, rather sinister-looking, dark, with pale faces, wearing overcoats, and went into an old kitchen? (I didn't see – just presumed it was a kitchen.) The kitchen (or whatever) was to the left. A little girl, sitting at a desk or table, to the right of the door was trying to tell me about a killing. I wouldn't let her say what she wanted to as I was frightened of the men.
>
> Very silently a woman passed me – I didn't notice her come in, she was so silent. She was fortyish, perhaps, short, very plain, insignificant, and quiet. Her hair was greyish, and drawn away from her forehead and face. She wore a mannish-type suit (skirt and jacket) which I think was grey. She had waxy looking skin on her face, a few or no wrinkles. The girl whispered to me 'She's the head of them', and I presumed that she meant that the woman was in charge of the operations. I was surprised, and thought 'You'd never guess it'.
>
> The little girl then told me that she and other children were only 'backward' children, not 'mental'. She kept reiterating 'backward' as if it was very important that I understood. She was trying to tell me the story about the 'killing', but I kept changing the subject so that the woman wouldn't hear the child.

That, then, was the dream. Mrs Goodsell's description of it is extremely good, conveying the amorphous nature and four-dimensional quality of so much dream content – for example, in dreams, one is so often *aware* of things which are not actually seen, and of interpreting motives, thoughts and actions without any 'visual' evidence to support them, as the dream flows or progresses. Mrs

Goodsell seems able to distinguish between, and to remember more clearly than most of us, what was seen or merely inferred, what was said, or thought to be said, within a dream.

The following morning Mrs Goodsell heard that a lot of children in a home for 'backward' children had been burned to death at Froissy, near Beauvais, in France.

The important coincidence here is that the school was for *retarded*, not *mental* children. The fourteen children died in a locked room when fire swept through the home. Rescue attempts proved impossible because of the dense smoke, and the victims were among fifty-nine children who were slow to learn, dulled in their perceptions, slow in their reflexes or physically ungainly. The home was a red-bricked, stone-faced manor-house.

It will be noted that only one part of this particular dream seems to have been precognitive. Mrs Goodsell had dreamed of a sense of menace from two men and an insignificant looking woman; of a killing rather than an accident; of a cottage rather than a manor-house. But that she should have dreamed of backward children at the time this tragedy was being enacted in a home for backward children is certainly interesting. Many of her dreams were more specific than this, embodying far more coincidental detail. But dreams do not have to be *wholly* precognitive to have either interest or significance, although obviously, they are of a greater interest when the variety of coincidental content is greater. Dreams constitute a seemingly incoherent mixture of past, present and future – the mind moved untrammelled backwards and forwards in time, sometimes 'projecting' future occurrences against a background of past memories, or vice versa. It is less frequent, though not unknown, for anyone to have, so to speak, a pre-run of the film they will see later – or which somebody else is destined to see later.

'There was nothing in that dream to tie up with the fire,' Mrs Goodsell told me, 'but the coincidence, in that I dreamed of retarded children, set me wondering whether that had been a case of telepathy, or whether in my dreams I was in fact getting glimpses of the future. The fire stimulated my interest in precognition; compared with later dreams, it was unimpressive, in that the sense of menace in my dream was confined to two gangster-like figures. But it had the useful purpose of getting me going in recording my dreams. It has to be done almost immediately after a dream has been experienced, as once vanished a dream can seldom be recalled.'

A more disturbing, and more markedly precognitive dream was experienced on the night of 24 June 1969 and duly recorded.

Mrs Goodsell told me:

> I dreamed I was on a kind of quay, queuing up to get into a 'tin' type of boat. Some of the details seem a bit vague now, but what wasn't vague, but insistent in the dream and my subsequent memory of it, was that the boat was of a 'tin' type and that there were a lot of children on board. It seemed to me in the dream that there was great danger, and my desperate concern was to get Cindy (my daughter) off the boat to safety. She was downstairs in the boat. There didn't appear to be any safety railings on the top deck and I was very worried about all the other children. In the next part of the dream, I was 'hovering' over the beach and I could see children floating in the water drowned or drowning. One child was a girl with long hair. I managed to 'magic' her out of the water and pumped her out. I was trying to attract the attention of other people who were sitting on the beach eating sandwiches. I wanted them to save the children I couldn't reach, but they seemed totally oblivious of the disaster that was happening. Little girls were floating in the water, one face down, another face up and the people ignored the whole episode as if it were not happening ...

This dream was to prove a frightening experience for Valerie Goodsell, and not merely because of its unpleasant content. She told me:

> I knew that it was one of 'those' dreams – one of those dreams with an element of fear about it that couldn't quite be put satisfactorily into words – and I couldn't understand it. The next day I was taking a party of school children from Kent on an outing by train, and couldn't

help wondering if my dream the previous day had been a portent or warning of some kind. It was impossible not to feel to some vague extent uneasy, and, as a natural reaction to that, to be just that little extra bit alert. Until now, all my dreams seemed to be re-enacted the following day, so that it could have been argued, as I argued with myself, that by some strange means I was 'picking up' telepathically what was happening elsewhere. If things were happening while I was dreaming about them, and I merely read the confirmation of it having happened in the newspapers the next day, it could, as I say, have been mere telepathy. But that morning I'd seen nothing in the papers about a boat sinking. I thought that the dream might have been a precognitive warning to take special care of the children on the train. Despite feeling worried throughout the day watching to see that nothing dire happened, everything went smoothly and we arrived back at the school quite safely, with nothing amiss.

You can imagine my shock when, on *30 June 1969*, a week later, there was a report in the papers of a new aluminium oyster boat that capsized in Galway Bay. The boat was carrying 48 people, mostly women and girls from the convent of Mercy College in Kinvarra. Three boys and five girls were drowned. This was the first dream I had had where I had dreamed the event a week *before* it happened.

The disaster of which Mrs Goodsell had a prevision occurred on Sunday 29 June 1969. The *Red Bank* capsized 150 yards off the village of New Quay while carrying children on a pleasure trip. It had already made five trips and had announced that this would be the last of the day – the day of its launching. One survivor described the panic on the boat when it took water over one side as it turned to go back to the pier. The crowd moved to one side, and the boat took more water before overturning.

The links between the dream and the actual occurrence are impressive. She had dreamed of a *quay* – the tragedy happened near New Quay. She dreamed of a line of children queuing up to get on to a 'tin' type of boat – the children, in fact, queued up to get on to an aluminium boat. She had seen children floating in the water or drowning.

One obvious question to ask, and of course I did ask it, was whether she made known the content of this dream before the tragedy was reported. 'I told my husband, because I was panic-stricken about taking those children to Bromley, and felt sure because of my dream – and so many had proved themselves almost immediately after dreaming – that something terrible was going to happen. I thought the dream was a presage of disaster. I was clucking about like a mother hen and they must have thought that I was crazy.'

Mrs Goodsell's first experience of precognition was at the age of eighteen. At this time she had been beset by a certain amount of nervous trouble. She had a dread of mixing with people, to such an extent that she would avoid a crowded bus home, and walk considerable distances to reach a train which was usually empty.

She was then living with her parents at Sevenoaks, in Kent, and as she walked towards the railway station, she became aware that she ought on no account to walk on any further. It wasn't a voice, in the accepted sense of the term, but a powerful thought, a specific impulse of an inhibiting kind – 'something other than me' was how she described it. 'Because I was in such a nervous state, I was cross with myself for being, as I supposed, stupid, but nevertheless I lingered for a while, looking into a very boring shop window, and was very reluctant to proceed further down the hill towards the station. I felt very silly, and regarded myself as a fool.'

In this state of self-reproach, she inwardly berated herself for lack of will power and common sense, decided to disregard what seemed to her to have been a powerful and urgent warning, and forced herself to trace her steps towards the station. She told me:

> I had just begun to walk down, when suddenly I heard an almighty crash of cars, the sound of smashing glass and then the silence that follows after. With my heart in my mouth, I walked on down, and just round the corner, where I surely *must* have been had I not stopped, three cars had collided into a wall, up on to the pavement, and had knocked down a pedestrian. The pavement at that stage is

narrow, with a high wall at the back of it, enabling no escape from a car in the event of such an accident. I could not stop shaking, not from my narrow escape, but because of the fact that somehow I had known that this was going to happen and had been warned not to go on. When I got home, white and shaken, I told my parents what had happened.

Early in 1975 the Goodsell family moved to Snettisham, near King's Lynn, on the east coast of England, and thereby hangs an interesting precognitive tale.

In 1973 Mrs Goodsell dreamed that she was at an auction sale. Meeting a man she asked him, 'Is this the auction', and he replied, 'Yes, this is your house.' She then saw the house itself with fair realism. She was inside it, looking up into the rafters, and could see that a dormer window was being put in. It seemed to be an old type of house, vaguely Gothic or 'churchified' and snow was falling. She told her husband the following morning that when they moved to a bigger place, it would have oddly shaped windows and they would have to move in winter.

In the event, they moved to a large building at Snettisham consisting of three cottages put together, with windows having a 'churchified' look, each with a sort of Gothic arch. It was fine and sunny on the day they moved, but within weeks winter had arrived, and snow was falling.

I noted many other examples of experiences which had in them an element of precognition, too numerous to relate here, and, like those I quoted, involving some degree of corroboration. Despite her early nervous troubles, which are usual enough in adolescence and beyond, and about which she is perfectly frank, I rate her a credible witness.

# 4 Prevision of Romance

In a pleasant Decimus Burton house in Calverley Park, near Tunbridge Wells in Kent, 'The Garden of England', Lady Dowding (full title, the Right Honourable Muriel, Lady Dowding), related to me the remarkable story of how she had 'seen' and spoken to her second husband long before they met.

Put in that matter-of-fact way, it would seem reasonable to remember that many women – like men – often have a mental picture, a sort of preconception based on instinctive preferences, of the person they would eventually *like* to marry and, later on, meeting such a person, they are drawn to them and see their wish fulfilled.

However, Lady Dowding's experience was not like that. Let me introduce the two main characters in this precognitive drama.

Lady Dowding is the widow of a war hero, Hugh Caswall Tremenheere Dowding (1882-1970), 1st Baron Dowding, and a British air marshal. As chief of Fighter Command, to which he was appointed in 1936, his magnificent leadership and abilities as a commander played a leading part in winning the Battle of Britain in 1940. He had helped not merely to save Britain when she was comparatively ill-equipped, but Europe itself, since the British Isles remained the only springboard from which a Nazi-enslaved Europe could be freed. He was tall, ascetic-looking, clear-thinking, courageous and with a tremendous sense of organization. As an observer, and later as a pilot on the Western Front, he had seen action in World War One with the Royal Flying Corps. During the thirties, as dictators Hitler and Mussolini engaged in a frantic arms build-up in preparation for World War Two, Dowding stood alone – except, perhaps for Winston Churchill – in maintaining that the prevailing apathy would be short-lived and that shortly Britain would face her greatest crisis of survival. He pressed for the production of small, manoeuvrable fighter planes, such as the Hurricane and the Spitfire. He resisted pressures to deplete his meagre fighting force for a hopeless last-minute attempt to retrieve lost ground in France. Only narrowly, thanks for his foresight and judgement, was Britain spared a Nazi invasion.

Lord Dowding retired soon after the Battle of Britain. He was a fervent Spiritualist, believing in the survival of human personality, in some form, after death.

Lady Dowding is best known for her campaign for the better treatment of animals, against vivisection, and for vegetarianism. Her father's surname was Albino (after his ancestor, D'Albini, who came over with William the Conqueror in 1066). Her father received so strict a religious upbringing that once he had freedom of choice he rebelled and became an agnostic, unlike his two brothers who became priests, or his older sister who was a Catholic missionary. To avoid being carried further on the religious roundabout, he had jumped the train on the way back with his family from a holiday in Scotland and married a Protestant girl whom he had met at a ball. Her upbringing had been equally strict, her father being the 1st, 2nd and 3rd Mayor of St Pancras and a solid pillar of the Protestant church. Lady Dowding's grandfather married an Irish woman, Mary Regan, who was reputed to be psychic, and it is from her, she believes, she probably inherited her own highly developed intuition and precognitive capacities.

Despite many proposals in her teens and twenties, Lady Dowding did not get married until the Second World War, when she fell in love with Pilot Officer Maxwell Whiting, who was killed in an air crash in 1944 while serving with Bomber Command. Theirs had been a brief, young, happy time together and she had no thought of marrying again.

She pursued her interest in Spiritualism and the occult and became secretary of Tunbridge Wells Theosophical Society, living with her son David in an old timbered house on a hilltop near Tunbridge.

Her first marriage, however, links in a most peculiar way with her second.

In October 1944, Mrs Maxwell Whiting – as she was then – was staying in Somerset. She had received a note from her husband saying: 'If you ever get this, it means that I have been unable to get back to you. But don't worry. Just as you are about to marry a millionaire, I shall turn up. If I am not able to do this, I will try to contact you through any of the sources you believe in.'

Naturally, in face of this last message, and believing as she did in human survival, Lady Dowding tried to contact him at a Spiritualist seance and at it, she maintains, her dead husband spoke to her. As a result, she discovered how he died, something which, at that time, was not even known to the authorities. She had assumed that because seventeen Lancaster bombers had failed to return from a bombing raid on Duigsburg (the Rhine port of Western Germany, in the Ruhr, centre of steel production, shipbuilding, engineering and armaments production) after which he had been reported missing, that he must have met his death over Germany. However, at the seance a message she received from a presence which she accepted as being that of her husband told her that his last memory was of *seeing the coast of Norway*.

To this assertion she replied, as she explained to me, 'Oh no, Max, you went to Duigsburg', to which his reply was, 'I assure you I did not. I will try and bring you evidence.' He added that he was passing over Denmark and flying towards the coast of Norway when German fighters came in after them. There was a brief moment when he said to himself, 'This is it', and the plane exploded. He described the sensation of dying – like falling down a huge tunnel at the far end of which a light could be seen.

The relevance of all this to our essential theme of precognition is that Maxwell Whiting was later proved right as to the manner of his death. A forecast he made concerning Lady Dowding's next marriage also proved accurate. There remained, however, the uncertainty as to the time, place and manner of her husband's death.

'Two years later,' she told me, 'that is, in 1946, my stepfather got chatting to a Dane in the course of a train journey. The war had only recently ended, and he had asked the Dane what conditions had been like in his country. The Dane replied, "Well, we had one very tragic experience. One of your Lancaster bombers crashed on my ground. I shall never forget that night of 22 May 1944".'

Her stepfather noted the date, as a result of which further enquiries were pursued. These showed that the Danes had erected a memorial to the gallant English airman, a photograph of which the Dane sent to the stepfather. This, passed on to the Air Ministry, enabled them to make further enquiries and to establish that the plane in question was indeed that in which Maxwell Whiting had crashed.

The information given to Lady Dowding before these enquiries, being accurate, could in one sense be termed precognition, in so far as she had received it from a mysterious source and in advance of the authorities. But whereas that information concerned *the past*, she was given at the same seance an accurate prediction of *the future*. Her dead husband had said that she would marry again, and that her next husband would be a much older man. 'It's a good thing,' the message said, 'that you like scrambled eggs.'

This last sentence made no sense to her, nor did she find it easy to believe that she would ever fall in love with an older man. 'Please don't talk about it,' she had said, to which the reply came 'It is what is to be. I am happy and proud, and it is what is meant.' As to the obscure reference to 'scrambled eggs', the puzzle was solved in an unexpected way. A year or so after her second marriage, a friend, looking at a photograph of her famous airman husband in the uniform of an Air Marshal said, 'Look at all that lovely scrambled egg.' She learned that this was the slang for all the gold braid of a high-ranking officer – so her first husband's strange remark about scrambled eggs was, Lady Dowding is convinced, his way of giving her a clue.

We now come to one of the most remarkable authenticated cases of precognition that it is possible to imagine.

It was 1944. The then Mrs Whiting was staying with two close friends (Joan Clarke and Brenda Bookman) in Somerset. She had her young son, David, with her and her two friends had children of about the same age.

Mrs Whiting had received the shattering telegram telling her of her husband's death in action: she was absolutely numbed by it.

> One day, I awoke in my bedroom, and standing in front of the mantelpiece was a tall, thin, grey-haired man with very blue eyes, wearing a blue shirt, black tie and grey flannel trousers.
>
> A curious feature of the dream, or vision or fantasy – whatever you care to call it – was that there were three model elephants on the mantelpiece (in actual fact, there were not) and he put one upon the back of another with such comical effect that I said 'Hugh, whatever are you doing?' and started laughing.

At this point her bedroom door opened, and her two friends looked in. Seeing her alone, and saying nothing further, they closed the door. At the moment they had opened the door the figure of the spare, grey-haired man had vanished.

What had happened is that her two friends woke up, went into the kitchen to have a cup of tea, to dress their boys, and get bathed and dressed and ready for the day. As they did so they heard voices coming from Muriel Whiting's room. Momentarily they thought Maxwell Whiting had come back on leave unexpectedly, until, sadly, they remembered that he was dead. Mrs Whiting had shown admirable self-control when that terrible telegram had arrived. She had made no scene, she had not even wept. Her grief, which they well understood must go deep, was concealed. Had she suddenly gone off her head? Had she cracked under the strain?

Dissembling their anxiety, they had dashed upstairs together, by which time they could hear their friend's laughter intermixed with voices. They opened the door and, seeing nothing in the room but their friend in bed, left again, puzzled and a little disturbed.

Later they put the question direct to her: 'Are you all right?'

'Yes', she replied.

'But who were you talking to?'

'I was talking to somebody called Hugh.'

'What was he like?'

'Grey-haired, tall and thin.'

Some weeks later when they were looking through some newspapers, which had just arrived, Mrs Whiting said 'You've asked me three or four times what Hugh was like – he was like *that* man (pointing to an illustration).'

'That is Air Chief Marshal Lord Dowding.'

Years later, when Mrs Whiting met Lord Dowding, she knew at once that he was the man she had seen, in vision, in her bedroom. He fell in love with her immediately. On that night in 1951 when they became engaged, the significance of that odd episode of the elephants in that 'vision encounter' in the cottage in Somerset years before was in a strange way revealed. 'We were to be married in a few weeks time,' Lady Dowding recalls, 'and Hugh kept phoning me up to say that we had better get some coal in. It really made me realize that we were going to get married, with a man telling me what to do in a domestic way. I suddenly realized that I had promised to go and have coffee with one of my neighbours. I rushed over rather late, apologising, and directly I went into her room, there were these elephants. I said, "Where did you get those from"? and she said, "They were given to me yesterday. Do you know what they mean? They mean happiness".'

Lady Dowding recalled: 'It came home to me that in my vision years ago, when Hugh was putting the elephants (which my friend, of course, hadn't got then) upon each other's backs, he did so in order that it might register with me.'

'Have you ever met me before?' Mrs Whiting asked him at their first meeting, with no indication of why she asked him. 'No,' he replied, 'I'm sure I'd have remembered if we had.'

When he put her on a train for Tunbridge Wells that day, she reflected that he was one of the nicest men she had ever met, yet doubted that she would ever see him again. In fact, they met frequently after that. On 25 September 1951, attended by only two witnesses, they married in London, at Caxton Hall. With characteristic modesty, Lord Dowding described himself as a widower of sixty-nine and a schoolmaster by profession. She was described merely as forty-three, widow of Pilot Officer Maxwell Whiting, of Bidborough, near Tunbridge Wells.

The final reminder that there is such a thing as precognition took Lady Dowding back to a long-distant childhood dream. In brilliant sun, she was being carried along in a royal procession, attended by coloured retainers and believing, in her dream, in the manner that one merely *knows*, that she was one of a number of concubines of a royal personage, with whom she was much in love. He had given her a bracelet, which he had placed upon her right wrist. It glistened brilliantly in the sun. It was a very vivid dream, and the memory of that bracelet remained with her.

The first gift that Lord Dowding ever gave her *was* a bracelet. It was over twenty years after she had seen it in her dream, marvelled at it coruscating in the sun, and now he produced it from his pocket.

'Have you ever given a woman a bracelet before?' she asked.

'No. You're the first,' he said.

She extended both wrists. He slipped the bracelet on her right wrist, just as it had been worn in her dream.

For nineteen years, until Lord Dowding died, they enjoyed, as Lady Dowding has put it, 'Great harmony, great physical and spiritual attraction. A really great love affair ...'

How and why did she see the man she was to marry, and did not then know, in that country cottage in Somerset, in 1944 – seven years before she married him?

# 5 The Weird Walk

In Longleat, the Wiltshire home of the Marquess of Bath, hangs a portrait by the American artist, John Singer Sargent. It is of the 5th Marchioness of Bath and was painted in 1913.

This tremendous mansion houses so many treasures, accumulated over the centuries, that the portrait, good as it is, attracts much less attention than many other features, such as the family portaits with their fantastic period costumes, the carvings of the Great Hall and the books and treasures worth over six million pounds.

As most people know, Longleat is one of the largest private residences in the world, and is visited by over 200,000 people every year. It has been the home of the Bath family for nearly four hundred years.

Like most stately homes, Longleat has its ghosts, such as Bishop Ken, who once came to dinner and stayed for twenty years in the huge, rambling library named after him, and Sir John Thynne, builder of Longleat and Lord Bath's ancestor, whose shade has been seen by several people, at different times, in the magnificent Red Library (so called because of the colour of its wall-covering), which houses one of the largest collections of books on the French Revolution. A German journalist, Guy Montag, once telephoned me during a visit to England to say that he wanted to sleep in a haunted place. I suggested Longleat and, the owners obliging, he spent the night in the Red Library and got the surprise and fright of his life, for the shade of Sir John appeared distinctly to him, and stayed several minutes.

But something equally weird, and even more inexplicable, transpired once at Longleat, on an occasion when time did not stand still, did not even regress as it seems to do when the shades of the past appear, seemingly alive and moving, centuries after their death; it was an occasion when the future unfolded, for no known reason and in accordance with no known laws. It was precognition in the truest sense, having nothing in common with the more common phenomenon of premonition. I am indebted to the Marquess of Bath for the facts of what I choose, reasonably I think, to call the weird walk.

> My mother, the 5th Marchioness, used to have dreams of a special nature, quite unlike ordinary dreams. She used to call them, 'like pictures in front of my eyes'. In January 1891, she dreamed that my sister Kathleen was about to be born. She turned to my father telling him to get a nurse as quickly as he could, to which he replied, 'I cannot – it is Good Friday.' Ultimately, however, he got one and she was a short, stout lady. Next morning she told the dream to my father.
>
> It so happened that Kathleen was really due to be born at the end of May, and my mother had engaged a tall, thin nurse. On 27 March, she suddenly realized that the baby was due to arrive and informed my father to that effect. He turned to her and 'Dear me, what a bore – it's Good Friday.' He was, however, able to get help. The next thing my mother knew was that the nurse coming into the room to look after her was the short, stout lady she had seen in her dream.

The Marchioness certainly had psychic or intuitive faculties of an unusual kind.

'On the morning of 13 February 1916,' Lord Bath recalls, 'she dreamed that she saw my eldest brother John, lying in a dugout with his head propped up on a pile of blankets. That very same day a telegram arrived to say that John had been killed and about a year later, the then Colonel of the Scots Greys (Colonel Collins), in which my brother was serving at the time of his death, came to visit my mother and described to her in detail how John died, ending up with the exact description of how my mother saw him lying in a dugout, where he had been taken after he had been shot.'

The other 'dream' – if dream it were – proved even more extraordinary, as though time was playing some crazy trick contrary to the laws of science and commonsense. But there is absolutely no question as to the facts, which are these:

The fifth Marchioness was a semi-invalid who used a pair of sticks to walk and joined the family at dinner after the soup, so as to shorten the period of having to sit at meals.

'She used to look after a fox terrier called Jack,' Lord Bath recalls, 'who actually belonged to my sister, Emma. My mother's rooms were on the ground floor in the south-west part of Longleat, and every evening she and Jack used to walk along from the south-west wing down the corridor towards the Red Library and into the dining-room where the family were already seated, eating their second course. During this meal Jack was always fed and consequently, when my mother came out of her bedroom, he used to rush on ahead in the hope of getting his meal a little earlier.'

One evening the accustomed routine took place. The Marchioness came out of her bedroom, her fox terrier rushed on ahead – but with a distinct difference this time. For when she turned into the long corridor leading to the dining-room, Jack came running towards her with his tail between his legs.

Puzzled, she looked down at her pet. 'What's the matter, old boy, seen spooks?' she joked, and stomped on down the corridor with her sticks.

She then noticed that she couldn't see the anteroom down at the far end of the passage, because a dust-sheet was hanging from the archway leading into the hall of the staircase.

'My mother,' said Lord Bath, 'thought this strange, since she had not noticed it when she went to dress for dinner, but assumed that the housemaids had decided that something needed cleaning and had put the sheet there to prevent the dust from spreading into the corridor.

When she arrived at the dust-sheet she took hold of it, pulled back the loose flap to one side and went through into the hall of the staircase. Here, again, she noticed that she was unable to see the anteroom because another dust-sheet was hung over the second archway. At the same time she had the feeling that there were a lot of people around her, not only on the floor of the hall, but up the staircase and there seemed to be a murmur of voices about her.

Still not worried, she went towards the second dust-sheet and once again stopped, pulled the loose flap to one side and began to pass through into the hall corridor. In order to avoid the dust-sheet, it was of course necessary to turn her head to one side and in so doing she noticed that Jack was pressing as hard as he could against the far side of the wall and as far away from the dust-sheet as possible.

My mother then began to realize that she had seen something which was not altogether ordinary, and with her heart beating somewhat faster than usual, she carried on down the corridor with her two sticks. But as she was about to open the anteroom door, she realized she was running away from a situation which was of absorbing interest to her, so she turned round and looked again. At that moment a housemaid came out of the passage and everything disappeared. My mother told me that she then lost no time in reaching the family dining-room (I myself was then too small to go down to dinner).

Later that night she told them all she had seen. That was in 1914.

In May 1916 a fire broke out at Longleat and burnt part of the wall in the hall from which the staircase ran. Luckily, owing to the presence of a paid fireman and the assistance of wounded soldiers who then occupied the house, the fire was put out with very little damage. My sister Kathleen was sitting in her room at the time when the alarm was given and later that morning went along to the hall and found that dust-sheets had been hung over the arches to stop the draught from spreading the fire to the rest of the house. She asked the firemen to be as quiet as they could as it would frighten Lady Bath who was not yet up, but after about half an hour my mother suddenly appeared, pulling the dust-sheet aside, saying "This is what I saw in my vision."

It was later discovered that the fire had been caused by a new central-heating system, which was being installed: a boiler placed too close to a beam had led to slow combustion and ultimately the fire. 'Thus,' says Lord Bath, 'when my mother passed that way that night, the very cause of the fire was, in fact, taking place under her feet.'

Why did the Marchioness see, two years ahead, the reality that came afterwards? Why was that experience so vivid that she recounted it, in detail, to her family?

It would seem that on occasions what we call 'time' did not operate at all with her as it does with most of us. Was it telepathy or precognition that informed her of the circumstances of her son John's death? And what of her experience of retrocognition (the reverse of precognition – the mind going *backwards* in time to an unfamiliar period). 'Once my mother was sleeping in the Dowager Rooms at Longleat and one night (she could not remember whether she was asleep or half-awake) a man with a peruke and a prune-coloured coat came towards her at the end of the bed and nodded at her. The man closely resembled the picture of the 1st Marquess now hanging over the chimney-piece in the downstairs dining-room. When she told the rest of the family what she had seen, everybody was very scornful, as the coat which he wore in the picture was depicted as black and not prune. A few years later, however, the picture was cleaned, and it was revealed that instead of the black coat, he was wearing a prune coat as seen by my mother when he appeared to her.'

Lord Bath's mother also claimed that the swans at Longleat told her, by their behaviour, what was going to happen. She set much store by such a phenomenon as three swans flying up the ponds and only two coming back. The behaviour of swans was, she believed, a presage of events to come, and the precedent she established remained with the family as a kind of tradition. For example, Lord Bath's sister, Emma Lady Northampton, was one day looking from her cottage (The Curatage) at Horninghsam, down towards the ponds when she noticed four swans flying away in the direction of Longleat. About half-way down, two of them separated, leaving the other two continuing on their flight. On entering the house she told her maid what she had seen and how worried she was. 'Do not worry, my lady,' the maid replied, 'they were too far away to affect you.' The very next day the two eldest sons of Lord Bath's sister, Kathleen, Lady Stanley, met with an accident while exploring some sand-dunes near Holyhead, on the Welsh coast, and were killed.

Certainly the 5th Marchioness of Bath was unusually prone to precognitive glimpses, not always, but frequently by means of dreams. Another concerned a dream in which she walked through a long, dark tunnel and emerged the other side to find her mother (who incidentally had died when she was a small child) in a beautiful garden. While she was there, she saw her aunt May come into the garden.

'My mother's mother', Lord Bath told me, 'took my mother by the hand and said "You had better go back now." In the dream her aunt was very blue in the face, and mother did duly 'go back'. That very same day, news came that Aunt May had died of cancer of the lung.'

It is characteristic of precognition that it can operate in respect of trivial as well as important matters. If the detail is unusual enough, its seeming unimportance does not detract from the essentially remarkable nature of the phenomena – whatever the *content* of the prevision, it is inherently extraordinary that it should happen at all.

Lord Bath recalls:

On one occasion, my mother told me that she heard the words in one of her dreams, 'The seat of the trouble lies behind the black cabinet in the upstairs drawing-room'. Naturally, such a trivial remark made no impression on her and I do not think that at the time she told anybody about it. However, a little later the chimney in the Green Library immediately below the drawing-room began to smoke very badly indeed, and Mr Hughes, who was then Clerk of

Works, was told to find out why. For about a week he looked all over the place and finally came to my mother and said 'I cannot find the cause of this chimney smoking.'

It was then that my mother remembered the words she had heard in her dream and she said, 'Would you do something to please me and look behind the black cabinet in the drawing-room upstairs, because I think you will find the trouble there.' The Clerk of Works said that in his opinion it was completely out of the question that the trouble could be there. But sure enough, when he opened up behind the black cabinet, there was the trouble, which to the best of my remembrance, was a displacement of one or two bricks lodged in the centre of the chimney.'

Lord Bath is convinced that some people do have a sixth sense and, through their dreams or otherwise, see into the future.

Of all the remarkable stories he is able to adduce about his mother, the most impressive is certainly that of the fire up the staircase at Longleat, for this strange 'waking vision' was vividly and accurately precognitive, since this was recorded by her *about two years before* the actual fire took place.

The frequency with which the 5th Marchioness saw into the future raises the vexed question of whether life is all mapped out for us. On this question, Lord Bath has no doubts whatsoever.

'It seems to me,' he says, 'that these dreams prove conclusively that fate must prevail even down to the smallest detail, in other words, in my opinion, free-will is non-existent in any shape or form whatsoever.'

# 6   A Distant Drum

A very strange letter arrived – in a sack-load of other mail – at the *Daily Mirror* office at 3.15 p.m. on 8 December 1954. The letter was typed. It was anonymous except for the initials 'G.S.'.

It read:

Dear Sir,

This is to advise that soon 'A GREAT Storm is coming. The wind will be as a CYCLONE.

It will bring disaster in its wake. This is NOT a joke. There is not much that can be done unless you advise your readers to take reasonable precautions with windows and doors, to see that the wind and the rain do not play havoc; or to take other storm precautions necessary which will suggest themselves to the individual; for some of the clearing of drains to carry the water would be a good idea.

I cannot at the moment tell you WHEN this will occur, only SOON.

Newspapers are used to receiving unusual letters. Many mark the beginning of enquiries which uncover sensational and important news stories. It might, the *Mirror* thought, be from a crank – but what was there to lose? They would merely keep the letter at hand and see if its prophecy was fulfilled. In this instance, they did not have long to wait. At five o'clock, less than two hours later, a whirlwind tore its way across London. Roofs were dislodged and sent flying through the air. The hurricane uprooted trees, tossed people and cars about, blew down a house and wrecked a station. The anonymous writer said that it would happen, and it did.

It later transpired that the correspondent was Mrs Gladys Saunders, a 45-year-old shorthand typist living in the suburb of Putney. As a person, there seemed nothing unusual about her. She was relaxed in demeanour, quietly spoken and full of sound common sense – not the sort of person one imagines would have psychic gifts.

What, then, impelled her to write that letter?

It seems that she was in the habit of receiving prior information of such happenings. In this instance, she had been sitting in front of the fire at home with her cat beside her when an 'inner voice' spoke quietly to her. The words which she had written to the *Daily Mirror* were exactly as she had received them.

That was an interesting case of precognition, though less detailed than some.

From Mrs Ralph H. Rose, of Hobart, New York, I have a very dramatic story of how the future was revealed in a very unusual way. That it happened long ago in no way detracts from its inherent interest. She told me:

> My mother had a precognitive dream just once in her lifetime, but it was a remarkable one for its great detail, which I can vouch for because she told me about the dream the morning after she had it.
>
> This happened some time between 1921 and 1924, while mother and I were living in an apartment in Denver, Colorado. A dry-land farm, which my father had operated until his death in 1919, at the time of the dream was occupied by a family called Shacklee. The farm was about three-and-a-half miles from the small village of Briggsdale in north-eastern Colorado. This was still rather pioneering country in some respects. Except along the State Road, the telephone service utilized the top wires of the barbed-wire fences, with the wires on elevated poles only to span the intersections of the roads; and the town was served by just one train each day ...
>
> For two or three years after my father's death, mother and I had operated the farm. Then we had sold at auction our livestock and personal effects and rented a place on shares to Mr Shacklee. At the time we were arranging

things for the auction, mother came to me with a new
pump rod, which still had attached to it the hardware
store's tag, and said: 'It seems a shame to sell this. It
probably will bring little or nothing. Some day probably we
will have to replace the pump rod at the well. We ought to
keep this safely put away somewhere.'

Between us, we decided to hide it on top of the
foundation wall of the house, under the cellar steps, where
no one would have any reason to look, and where
darkness would conceal it from view. Neither of us
mentioned it to anyone.

One Sunday morning at breakfast, mother said to me, 'I
am just worn out – as if I hadn't had a wink of sleep. I had
such a disturbing dream last night, and when I woke up
my heart was pounding and I was so worried. I turned
over on the other side and went back to sleep, and didn't I
go and dream the whole rigmarole over again!' I said: 'Tell
me your dream, and that will get it off your mind'.

Thus did her mother unburden herself of the whole
detailed, disturbing nightmare, so vivid that the morning
light and diurnal round of duties ahead could not dispel it
from her mind.

She dreamed that she was riding on the wagon seat of a
double-box (high-sided) wagon, seated beside a man she
did not know, who was driving. He was a very large man,
and there was something strange about the side of his
face, but she didn't know just what.

They were approaching the entrance road to our farm and
the barbed wire gate was open. As they turned in, my mother
was shocked to see things were in a terrible shape. Part of the
barn roof had gone; some of the buildings, including the
house, had windows broken out; the big machine shed was
shifted off its foundation and she could not see the chicken
house at all. The place was littered with shingles and broken
boards, and curled and bent pieces of old corrugated iron,
some of this litter even lying over an adjoining field.

As they came in, she saw Mr Shacklee and two other
men standing by the well, and he came towards her, and
she still sat in the wagon, and 'I'm glad to see you, Mrs
Eisnor. We are just repairing the windmill, and I notice the
pump rod is just about worn out. We might as well put in a

new one while we have things disconnected. If you'll OK it, I'll drive to town and get a new one right away'.

She said: 'There is a new pump rod. It's on top of the cement foundation under the cellar steps.'

In her dream she did not see him go to get it, but he said to her, 'I looked there, and I can't find any pump rod.'

She told him 'Feel way back – it's far back.'

Then he went to the house, and the driver of the wagon helped her down from the wagon and drove away. Mr Shacklee came back again, 'I sure can't find it. You must be mistaken.'

So Mrs Eisnor went into the house, made for the cellar stairway, where there were several wooden boxes, stood on one of them and felt in the place where she and her daughter had left the pump rod. It was gone.

Mrs Eisnor awoke, depressed and upset with the hangover of foreboding that such dreams can leave – not merely the deplorable state of the farm in which she had spent so much of her life, but at the thought that, in her absence, somebody might be stealing things from her.

Nowadays it might seem much ado about a pump rod, but in a remote spot such as Briggsdale it was mightily important as a means of drawing upon a source of water. If one needed a pump rod, nothing but a pump rod would do.

As the dream continued to prey upon her mind, she turned to other matters and after two days had elapsed the sense of foreboding lifted.

Then a letter arrived from Mr Shacklee saying, in effect, that they had experienced a terrible hurricane. 'Everything', he wrote, 'is in a pretty sad condition. Some things I know must be taken care of right away, so I am repairing those without waiting to hear from you. But I think you should try and come up as soon as you can, to see the condition of buildings and so on, and to tell me what you want me to do about them.'

Strangely, the arrival of the letter did not recall the dream to either of them. They were too involved with the immediate problems the storm had created, with the business of getting some money from the bank for urgent disbursements, and with packing what she would need to take with her.

Mrs Eisnor took the train to Briggsdale, but had not written to Mr Shacklee, assuming that she would be able to telephone him upon arrival, and that he would come down in his car and fetch her. But when she got to the town it was impossible to telephone, as telephone poles, fences and most other things were blown down, or damaged and service was suspended. She consulted an old friend, the local postmaster, who said he would try and find somebody to drive her out.

In a short while he introduced her to a tall, heavily built man with a very red face and a deep scar along one cheek, which somewhat disfigured his mouth on that side. He looked vaguely familiar to her and she tried to place him, but Mr Wilson the postmaster said that he was a newcomer to the state. The man said he had bought a farm some miles beyond hers, and would drop her off at the Shacklees' place on his way home from town. He asked her if she thought she could get on to a double-box wagon if he helped her. 'I was able to', she told him, 'a few years ago, all by myself. So I suppose I can!'

From then on everything transpired exactly as in the dream she had related. It was like seeing the same film twice. The box-wagon and the man with the scar were coincidental; but every other detail was true. When she searched for the pump rod under the cellar stairs she had a strange, giddy feeling. 'It's the strangest thing', she told Mr Shacklee, 'I dreamed all this the other night. And I dreamed I couldn't find the rod, either. But I know it's there, and I'll be able to find it all right.' The boxes weren't there, as in the dream, but he fetched one for her to stand on, explaining that he always used to keep the boxes underneath the steps and had only carried them away the other day.

Understandably, Mrs Rose has often thought of her mother's strange experience and, try as she may, can find no answer to it. 'I hate to believe it,' she told me, 'But the only plausible explanation is that she was indeed 'displaced in time', and that in that other time-world, what was soon to happen here on earth, was already an existing reality.'

Whatever the merits of her hypothesis, the facts are certainly interesting and, in fact, the phrase 'displaced in time' is rather expressive. Such an experience can be very disturbing, and often it is impossible for the person who experiences the phenomenon to convince anyone else that it happened at all, as in the case of an ex-RAF officer I know who once found that several hours had 'disappeared' from his life, as though a period of time had elapsed without him being aware of it. It was vaguely comparable to the loss of continuity of the patient under an anaesthetic. One moment he is lying on his back waiting for an operation, exchanging banalities with the surgeon who is merely waiting to see that the anaesthetic has had its effect, and then, in *what seems* like a split second, he awakens to find everything has been done, and that, in what seems to him like a second's oblivion, a whole lot of things have been happening.

# 7  Displaced in Time

A catalogue of fear, should anyone be so morbid or foolhardy as to attempt to compile it, would be astronomical in its extent, and incredible in its diversity. Yet of all the terrifying experiences one can imagine, that of being lost in space must be one of the worst. Imagine the quandary of the astronauts who, a few years ago, found that through a technical fault their fuel was going to waste on the return journey from the moon! Parts of the rocket even drifted away. Supposing, on a brief 'space walk' an astronaut became detached? He would float in the void until he breathed his last, alone, amidst illimitable space.

Yet to be displaced in time, although a briefer, less hazardous and certainly more usual experience, can also be rather startling. Reaction to the experience, naturally, depends to a great extent on the temperament of the person concerned. The whole business of life, of adaptation to environment, demands that we become accustomed to risk and change, and remain to some extent equal to shock, stress and surprise. Some are puzzled, others bewildered, a few actually frightened – if not at the time, perhaps later when the weird and inexplicable nature of their recent experiences has at last really registered in all its implications.

Mrs Ruth Browning, of Disraeli Road, Ealing, London, is now in her seventies, and in excellent health. Her memory is vigorous, and she has, in particular, two vivid memories which she disclosed to me.

Some years ago (in the sixties), she and her daughter June were attending an athletic display at White City

Stadium. Her daughter was marking results on her programme as they became available, but this was sometimes difficult when more than one contest was in operation simultaneously. Being particularly interested in the high jump, which was taking place at the same time as the long distance running race, she managed to note the results of the former but not the latter.

'I missed the running – who won, and what were their times?' June asked her mother.

'Don't worry,' Mrs Browning replied – and without further ado gave her the names of the first, second and third winners and the times of the first and third (but not the time of the second). The seats being fairly close, and her voice carrying somewhat, a clergyman who was seated a few rows in front of them turned round and stared at Mrs Browning very intently. 'I thought he was looking at me with reproach or disapproval, perhaps because I was talking and upsetting his concentration,' Mrs Browning told me, 'and felt vaguely put out about it. It was the first athletic meeting I had attended, and I did not think that a reasonable amount of talk would matter.'

The races continued, and presently June said: 'I've made a mistake and filled in the wrong running race.'

The clergyman again turned and said to her, *'No, you did not make a mistake. Your mother gave you the correct names and times to a race which had not yet been run!'* He then gave her the correct answer to the race she had missed in giving the 'precognitized' results of the race yet to be. The clergyman understandably was very interested in this 'time slip'. When he had turned round and stared at her in the first place, it had been on the tip of his tongue to tell her that she had given her daughter the wrong results of the race under discussion. However, he felt this information might be taken amiss; although he was also extremely puzzled as to why anyone with such a good seat and view should get the results so diametrically wrong. That they related to a *later* race was soon apparent.

On another occason, while watching a sports event on the television at home, together with her husband, her cousin and his wife, a hurdle race was in progress.

Spontaneously she said: 'Isn't it a pity that that man, so far in front, should fall at the last hurdle and lose the race!'

Her cousin said, 'Don't be silly, the race is being run *now* – it's not a recording or a repeat.' Even as she spoke, the last hurdle was reached. The leader fell and lost the race.

Mrs Barbara Lee Bennett, of Albany Street, London, has had some decidedly dramatic experiences of time displaced.

Her first was as a young girl. A brand-new cinema – the first ever in the town – had been built, and opened in High Wycombe, now a largely industrial town with only a few old buildings left. But in her day it still retained much of its old character and the introduction of a Kinematographic theatre, or cinema, was a startling precedent. Mrs Bennett was given permission to go to the cinema and arranged to go with another small friend. They were near the entrance when she changed her mind. 'I'm not going in', she said, emphatically, 'it's going to fall down!' Her friend didn't know *why* she was supposed to believe such an extraordinary prediction, but reluctantly accepted it, perhaps because she did not want to be left alone. The two spent the day by the river instead. And – yes, brand-new cinema though it was, and long before the jerry-built era of over-large floors and ceilings – the cinema *did* fall down. Not that afternoon, fortunately, but shortly afterwards, when it was empty.

In the ensuing years, Mrs Bennett was conscious of certain propensities which we would, I suppose, call 'psychic'. She made no hobby or special interest of such things. She merely found herself on the receiving end of strange experiences.

In the First World War her father, who had survived some of the bitterest fighting during the terrible battles of Paeschendale and the Somme, was eventually killed in action. She had made a habit of visiting Victoria station for the incoming trains bringing home the wounded, but on one occasion she did not go. She *knew* he had been killed and awaited the formal telegram.

On some occasions, Mrs Bennett is convinced that she has seen him, and even spoken to him. 'Take care of the

Goadie', she once heard him say, the old term for the
Collie and Cattle dogs.

During the Second World War, Mrs Bennett's husband
was a heavy rescue squad rescue leader with the Air Raid
Precautions organization. He and his wife were living at
the time in Agar Grove House, Camden Town, having
evacuated their five children to the country for safety from
air raids.

During the 1941 Blitz, Camden Town suffered very
heavily from air raids. There was a surface shelter in their
garden, which Mrs Bennett sometimes used. Such shelters
never afforded protection against anything more serious
than blast. There was an intensive cascade of fire bombs,
oil bombs, land-mines and high explosive bombs that
rained upon London, hour after hour, at the height of the
Blitz. Mrs Bennett, at her husband's insistence, sought
shelter in the underground.

One night, Mrs Bennett was on the way to Camden
Town station to try and get a little sleep, for the nights had
made sleep impossible with the continued thud and
crunch of bombs, the whine of shrapnel and the thunder
roar of the ack-ack guns. In the blacked-out street, as she
neared the station, she saw the shadow of her father in the
khaki uniform of the First World War. She heard him call
to her. Then she saw him nearer, with a large collie dog.
'Go home, sleep in your bed,' he urged, 'I am near you.'

Without hesitation, Mrs Bennett returned home and
went to bed in the garden shelter. That was the night that
bombs fell *into* Camden Town underground station,
causing fearful carnage amongst those who had taken
refuge there. Mr Bennett, who was called there with his
team to deal with the situation, was fairly beside himself
with grief and worry, thinking, as he applied himself to
rescue work, that his own wife might be there. The
casualties were horrifying – he went to pick up one
soldier, whose head rolled away.

Sick with worry, wearied with the night's work, Mr
Bennett returned home to find his wife alive and well –
thanks to the strange warning she had received and acted
upon.

When the mind, or soul, or spirit (all these are abstract terms lacking a precise meaning, but I mean by them, 'that self which is separate from, yet complementary to, the body') gets displaced in time, bizarre or comic or tragic experiences often ensue. Some phlegmatic types are merely curious. Others are frightened that a disclosure of their experiences to friends or relatives will earn them the reputation of being unbalanced or (in the case of those who might otherwise tell their workmates) of being unsuited to the discharge of their duties.

Fortunately, others are less diffident, or we should lack much fascinating evidence of the mutability of time. Consider this case, from the *Proceedings of the Society for Psychical Research*, Vol. X, p.332:

> Being at length tired, I sat down to rest upon a rock at the edge of the water. My attention was quite taken up with the extreme beauty of the scene before me. There was not a sound or movement except the soft ripple of water on the sand at my feet. Presently I felt a cold chill creep through me, and a curious stiffness of my limbs, as if I could not move, though wishing to do so. I felt frightened, yet chained to the spot, and as if impelled to stare at the water straight in front of me. Gradually a black cloud seemed to rise, and in the midst of it I saw a tall man, in a suit of tweed, jump into the water and sink.
>
> In a moment the darkness was gone, and I again became sensible of the heat and the sunshine, but I was awed and felt eerie – it was then about four o'clock or so – I cannot remember the exact time or date. On my sister's arrival I told her of the occurrence; she was surprised, but inclined to laugh at it. When we got home I told my brother; he treated the subject in much the same manner. However, about a week afterwards, a Mr Espie, a bank clerk (unknown to me) committed suicide by drowning in that very spot. He left a letter for his wife, indicating that he had for some time contemplated death. My sister's memory of the event is the only evidence I can give. I did not see the account of the inquest at the time, and did not mention my strange experience to anyone saving my sister and brother.

Thus a suicide was witnessed a week before it happened. How could this be?

Here is a classic case where several phenomena merge one into another. As I have long ago emphasized, in an earlier book, *Ghosts and Hauntings* (The Zeus Press, 1965) phantasms of the living are more common than those of the dead. Again, phantasms of the living also seem, on occasions, to have a telepathic origin – somehow somebody, somewhere, picks up in visual or audial form the thoughts of another person, possibly one far away. Was Mr Espie, who is known to have contemplated suicide at this spot for some time, thinking of his last act at the very moment that the other man was sitting at the edge of the water? Did the witness pick up, by telepathy, the thoughts in the mind of the suicide-to-be, and were these thoughts 'translated' into visual form?

The hypothesis is as complicated as it is unprovable. If the hypothesis is not accepted, had the witness seen into the future? How did he come to witness something that *was yet to happen* at that very spot?

This case was a corroborated one, and emphasizes the baffling nature of precognition.

To digress briefly – precognition and telepathy seem often related. Thoughts of the past, present and future are projected in some unknown way, both between humans and animals. When the Earl of Southampton was imprisoned in the Tower of London by Queen Elizabeth I for supporting the rebellion of the Earl of Essex, he was astounded when his favourite cat came tumbling down the chimney into his cell. How did the cat know where to find him? How did it know which chimney to choose? The mystified Earl had a portrait painted of himself, showing the inscrutable cat sitting contentedly on the window sill.

Mrs Carol Leong, of Brockwell, Chesterfeld, Derbyshire, has on several occasions found herself the victim of 'tricks of time'. On one occasion she found herself suddenly backwards in time:

I remember it vividly, despite the fact that I was only

fourteen at the time, simply for the sense of unreality and
horror it left me in. I was journeying on the bus to school,
going down Abbey Lane in Sheffield and travelled along
and up Hutcliffe Wood Road, got off the bus at Archer
Road, walked round the corner and got on the 45 trolley
bus. Noting the passage of the journey past the Endcliffe
Woods and Twentywell Section where the sun was shining
brilliantly; got off the trolley bus at Tolleybrook Road and
walked the rest of the half mile to school in bright sunlight
and arrived at school just as the bell was ringing. *It was the
bell which was the key factor, for I found myself still sitting in the
bus in Abbey Lane, but feeling almost exhausted. I am convinced
that I made that journey twice that morning, although I cannot
express the experience in more specific terms. The only thing that
I recall concerning my reactions was that I went cold and sticky
with horror, despite the fact that it was a hot summer's morning.*

Mrs Leong (then, of course, a young girl) had arrived at
the school and then found herself, so to speak, jerked
backwards in time to a previous stage of her journey. One
can well imagine the fright of such an experience.

Later – four years later – she was to find herself the
victim of another trick of time … On this occasion she 'lost
time':

I was eighteen years old and the experience still brings me
into gooseflesh just thinking about it. I had joined my two
aunts for the summer holidays and was living with my
aunt Eveline at Fords Cross and walking the two-and-a-
half miles to my Aunt Mildred's farm every day to
Stockland to help with the rook shoot (I'm an excellent
shot from youth).

Every morning I journeyed back up the hill to Claypitt
Cross, then down the steep-banked Devon Lane to a
junction in the lanes and took the right fork which passed
on the left a very high-walled farmyard now deserted, and
on the right, a very old wall with ivy and overhung with
elderberry. At the bottom of this lane there was a stream,
and one had to veer to the left in order to cross a narrow
wooden footbridge and thence for another quarter of a
mile up the last steep bit to Ford Cross.

The evenings were glorious, but the downward narrow

stretch to the stream was always cold and forbidding, and by the time I reached the stream always covered by a swirling low mist, my flesh was positively creeping.

On the last evening of the rook shoot my uncle accompanied me as far as Claypitt Cross, and when he and my cousin turned homeward I began to shake visibly with the terror of approaching this section. It was a beautiful night, and I began to wonder at the stars and the beauty of the crimson sunset, and I thought to myself that if all this was created by God that we must be thankful, for no matter what may happen to us, we had been given truly wonderful things to share in our lives and as I stopped thinking these thoughts *I was already walking up the upward hill of the last quarter of a mile to Ford Cross. I tried and tried to recall having walked through the section which I feared, and from which it was impossible to see the sky through the overhanging walls and trees, but I could not even recall walking over the bridge.* I cannot explain it at all. I am by nature both a curious and practical person and in all the experiences I have had which appeared to have some mystery, I eventually always found some credible answer apart from these two. Why did I not experience the physical temperature change of the water, which obviously accounted for the mist, but why did the mist never rise with the warmer air which must have been above it? ... Before I left my aunt's house I plucked up enough courage to ask her about it, and she said that the large right-hand wall had been part of a monastery and that a little farther away there was a priory, and that the babies born of this were drowned in the river – the stream I had to cross ...

Mrs Leong is at Chesterfield College of Technology. English by birth – on her mother's side, the well-known Lincolnshire family of Waddingtons (her grandfather was a Sheffield cutler), and on her father's side they were mostly farmers. As she claims quite truthfully, and I have observed, she combines a strong practical sense with a sensitive and imaginative response to the world she lives in – an integrated blend of common sense and mental curiosity, without which education has little real meaning.

Her husband is Chinese, and for a while she helped him with his considerable catering business in Singapore, then elected to return to England to continue her education at

Bristol University. She has no obvious quirk or phobias, and combines the exacting role of teacher with the upbringing of her four children. She speaks five languages, with smatterings of very many more tongues, and boasts a pleasantly contrasted range of hobbies and interests – art, breeding tropical fish, dog-showing, archaeology, writing poetry, writing travelogues and shooting.

All these presuppose a cool head and a fair nerve – not to mention a more than average amount of energy and drive – and I place her credibility very high indeed.

I asked her: 'Reverting to your strange experience, when you found yourself back on the 45 trolley bus, after you had already arrived at school in time for the ringing of the bell – could that have been a sort of day-dream?'

Mrs Leong is emphatic that it was *not* a day-dream, nor a case of amnesia. In fact, by a curious coincidence, she recently met an old lady who had experienced the selfsame thing: 'She lives in Chesterfield, and she asked me if I had ever left myself behind, so to speak. I knew what she was talking about, and when I told her of my experience she described a very similar thing which happened to her in 1929.'

Carol Leong assures me that there was a *reality* about the whole thing, like an eerie nightmare turned to fact. 'I was', she recalls, 'very, very shaken. Taken out of context it seemed absolutely logical, but put back into its context, it made very little sense. I am a very logical person, but whichever way I looked at it, I could find no explanation. There was no day-dreaming or dozing.' At this point we were discussing the 'back to the trolley bus'.

The experience of 'lost time' (my description for the sake of convenience, and implying no explanation on my part) at Claypitt Cross was equally terrifying. 'It wasn't as if I had been carried forward on the wind,' she explained to me, 'but rather that it simply wasn't in my mind. The ten or fifteen minutes it would have taken me – whatever had happened? Even talking about it now, turns me to goose-pimples – turns me quite cold.'

Just as Carol Leong is of logical disposition and practical

capabilities, having achieved the certificate of the Institute of Personnel Management, and the Further Education Training Certificate (not awards granted for undisciplined imagination), so Stuart Andrews, Sales Manager of Redheads, is the last person one would expect to be caught up in strange time-space experiences. But so it proved, and it is precisely his down-to-earth approach to living, and the continued round of practical problems he has to solve, that give his accounts special interest. At all times he answered my questions factually and readily, going to considerable trouble to consult diaries and notebooks, and supply names and addresses of those who could corroborate his statements. Some of his experiences fit into another context later on, but one seems to have been another example of 'time displacment', or perhaps, merely 'time vanished'.

During World War Two, Mr Andrews was at first a fitter-gunner and later an air-gunner with the Royal Air Force. He was stationed in the Sinai Desert, about fifteen kilometres outside Gaza, and was on guard duty from midnight until two o'clock in the morning.

He told me: 'I walked over to the fire in the centre of the camp which we kept burning, and we fired every ten minutes into the air to keep away any Arabs who might have crept up on the camp during the night, and as I walked over to the fire, somebody tapped me on the shoulder and said, "I'm your relief." It was 2.15 in the morning. Two hours of my life had gone by, and I most certainly wasn't asleep. I was not even tired – it wasn't worth while going to bed before midnight because one knew one had to be on guard.'

That was it. One moment he had gone on guard. The next moment, seemingly, he was relieved of duty, two hours, of which he had not the slightest consciousness, having elapsed.

Are the ghosts that so many people see a journey back in time, rather than an echo of the past, or a 'photoprint' of some tense emotional drama or dramatic event? Just as Carol Leong found herself jerked *backwards* into a trolley bus, and *forwards* through a section where the sky should have been invisible, but in fact was observed all the while, so, over sixty years ago, two highly respectable ladies whose story has since become an oft-quoted classic of its kind, found themselves whisked back into a past era, centuries ago.

Miss C.A.E. Moberley and Miss E.F. Jourdain, who were respectively Principal and Vice-Principal of St Hugh's College, Oxford, recounted in a book *An Adventure* (Aquarian Press, 1988) in 1911 how, on a visit to the Petit Trianon in Versailles in 1901, they found themselves wandering in gardens, not as they were in 1901, but exactly as they had been in the time of Marie Antoinette *a century and a half before*!

Strolling around, they met no less than eight people whose dress, demeanour and make-up belonged to the period of Marie Antoinette, and even the palace and grounds looked quite different from what they afterwards discovered to be the reality. Subsequent researches in the Bibliothèque Nationale established that they had both witnessed life in the Petit Trianon *as it was*, that they had by some amazing and inexplicable means been transported back in time. Many experts and specialists have looked critically at their detailed joint account (for example, the *Journal* of the Society for Psychical Research, p.178, 1950 and p.117, 1953) but the affair is as great a mystery today as it was then.

# 8   Time and Flight

Between precognition and aviation – in which, however inaccurately, I include space travel – there is a mysterious link.

Aviators have often remarked upon the sense of mystery, even of *presence*, they have felt on long, lovely flights or in moments of danger. It is not an easy thing to define. As the late Sheila Scott, the aviatrix who made innumerable record-breaking solo flights, told me: 'There's one thing about flying. It increases all your sensations and makes one tremendously alert. One is conscious of *something* mysterious in all that space – one doesn't know what it is, but it is real enough.'

It is this 'something' which, on one particularly perilous Atlantic flight (which, in defiance of established superstitions, she began on Friday the 13th, wearing green) the navigational controls went out of commission and for much of the flight over the Atlantic she hadn't the least idea where she was. Ice had forced her to fly well below 2,000 feet all the way, below 500 feet much of the way and at times as low as 50 feet above the sea. And as much of the waves were nearly 50 feet high anyway, the auto-pilot couldn't work in any case.

Despite tremendous headwinds, bitter cold and shortage of fuel, she managed to make Gander airport. It is largely instinct, training, courage – and this sense of identity with great but unidentifiable forces inherent in space and time, of which those who get away from the Earth's surface, including astronauts, are so acutely aware.

The immensity of what we vaguely conceive of when we talk of time *must* be acknowledged, if not grasped, if we are to get anywhere at all in our exploration of the implications and nature of precognition. Examples of foreknowledge are, strictly speaking, mere symptoms, minor manifestations of a prevailing state. It is many years indeed since I first read *The Story of Mankind* (Harrap, 1922) by the Dutch historian Hendrik van Loon, a masterly, popular condensation of history whose style and impact he was never again to equal in his subsequent works. There was about it a passionate simplicity and childlike awe in face of the marvel and mystery of life, the universe and human destiny which made a profound impression upon me, not least his masterly definition of time:

> High up in the North in a land called Svithjod, there stands a rock. It is a hundred miles high and a hundred miles wide. Once every thousand years a little bird comes to this rock to sharpen its beak. When the rock has been thus worn away, then a single day of eternity will have gone by.

Not a scientific definition of time, perhaps, but symbolic and descriptive.

Next, to the vastness of the universe, of which time is an inherent component, with space. Sir James Jeans (1877-1946), the English astronomer, mathematician and physicist, who developed the tidal theory of the solar system with H.A. Jeffreys, put it this way in *The Mysterious Universe*:

> A few stars are known which are hardly bigger than the earth, but the majority are so large that hundreds of thousands of earths could be packed inside each and leave room to spare; here and there we come upon a giant star large enough to contain millions of millions of earths. And the total number of stars in the universe is probably something like the total numbers of grains of sand on all the sea shores of the world. Such is the littleness of our home in space when measured up against the total substance of the universe.

For many years I have made a special study of precognition, and cases of foreknowledge, from people of undoubted probity and objectivity, have been collected from very many countries. I owe a good deal of encouragement in this work to the late Eileen J. Garrett, the English medium who settled in America and eventually founded the Parapsychology Foundation, an academically orientated organization which encourages research into these mysterious subjects in many countries.

The hundreds of accounts which I have collected are remarkable for the number of times aviation and flying come into it. Level-headed technicians, pilots and others whose work demands an ever-vigilant practicality often come face-to-face with weird phenomena which cannot be explained scientifically. Retrocognition and precognition do occur.

On a tour of British Army on the Rhine bases in Germany in the sixties, I stayed in Celle, on the site of the old Belsen concentration camp, and while there I visited the mass graves which remain as reminders of that endless slaughter and incredible inhumanity under Hitler. At one time smoke poured continually from the chimneys of the cremation plants in the camp, where thousands were killed every day, enveloping the beautiful village nearby with its greasy, noxious fumes. Yet an RAF pilot who flew me around, told me that on a flight over Celle he had seen the huge billowing wafts of smoke emerging from the oven chimneys dispersing in the summer sunshine. He later found that it was a sheer illusion, trained though his powers of observation are, and real though it had all seemed. He had seen from the air Belsen as it was *sixteen years before*!

'I have never fully trusted my senses since,' he told me. 'People may say it was an illusion. I don't believe any illusion can be as distinct and definite as that. For about ten minutes I was back in the past – don't ask me why, or how'.

Such experiences can be deeply puzzling. Just as this young pilot had found himself *back* in time, the late Air Marshal Sir Victor Goddard found himself, in the course of flying, *forward* in time. Fortunately he made detailed notes of all the circumstances, embodying these in an account, *Breaking the Time Barrier*, which he published in *Light*, the journal of the College of Psychic Studies, in 1966.

Sir Victor, then a staff officer in charge of operations of

No.3 Bomber Group, RAF had in 1935 been staying with friends in North Berwick for the weekend, having flown up in a Service aeroplane from Andover (where he was then stationed). It was a private flight, but aviation was still rather in its infancy, and the broad view was that the more flying an airman had, official or not, the better for his training and experience. This weekend jaunt was to involve an experience which Sir Victor Goddard hadn't bargained for and was thereafter never able to explain.

It occurred to Sir Victor that on a future visit to his friend, it might be possible to land his small aircraft at an old disused airfield at Drem, whose facilities and situation he remembered from World War I. There were still many such installations and buildings dotted about Britain, erected in a hurry and swiftly forgotten once the war was over. He went over to inspect the old airfield, with the permission of the farmer on whose land it was placed, with his hostess Mrs Peploe.

The place as he found it was certainly unusable. It was wholly neglected and gone to seed. Although there were four hangars laid out in line, three sets of double hangars and one single, the roofs were falling in. The tarmac was in 'sad disrepair' and a series of barbed-wire fences now divided the area into small separate pastures, in which animals were grazing.

So much for Goddard's hopes of an improvised airfield. The following morning he drove to Turnhouse (now Edinburgh airport) where he had left his Hawker Hart aeroplane. It was no weather for flying over mountainous territory in an open aircraft, without radio navigational aids or cloud-flying instruments, but he was young and tough and confident; clouds and rain notwithstanding, he decided to fly between a 'sandwich' of upper and lower clouds.

He was soon in trouble. His assumption of a gap in the cloud strata was wrong. Clouds persisted to a height of 8,000 feet; soon he was out of control and coming down in a spiral. He realized that it need not be disastrous; he knew how to make the spiralling faster or slower, but he could not correct the actual spiralling, and needed vision – soon –

to emerge without disaster.

Even at 1,000 feet he was still enveloped in cloud, rain and mist – indeed, it was darker. The clouds had become yellowish-brown and drenching with rain. (Goddard, of course, was himself drenched and frozen.) At a hundred feet he came into a hazy light and found himself over the Firth of Forth.

With desperate self-control he narrowly escaped death at this level – sea wall, paths, railings, a high stone wall. A startled girl, running in the pouring rain with a pram, had to duck her head to miss his wingtip.

Which side of the Firth of Forth was he? He wasn't sure, and with his compass swinging wildly, and forced to fly at the crazy height of twenty to thirty feet because of the extreme low-lying cloud, he searched for a landmark from which to orientate himself. Of course – Drem airfield! Where was that old airfield? He was, by the way, flying at 150 miles per hour. Soon he spotted the road to Edinburgh and ahead loomed the silhouettes of Drem hangars.

He then flew into the strangest episode of his life. As he came over the airfield, all the surroudings were bathed in sunlight. The rain had ceased. There were the hangars, their north-western doors wide open. In perfect order, on a brand-new tarmac, were four aeroplanes, whose details he noted with his clear and critical aviator's eye – three biplanes of a standard flying-training type known as Avro 504N and a monoplane of an unknown type.

But at this time there were no monoplanes in the RAF. Goddard carried the design in his memory and identified it years later as a 'trainer' that was later introduced and called the Magister.

Furthermore, *the aeroplanes he saw beneath him were painted bright yellow*, something he had never seen before. At that time (1935), trainer-planes were *silver*-painted. Not until 1938, when, with World War II imminent and expansion of the RAF being rushed ahead, so many trainee pilots were having fatal accidents, did the RAF switch to yellow paint for their trainer-planes so that they could more readily be identified.

Goddard noted another monoplane being wheeled out

of a hangar. The mechanics engaged in this task *were wearing blue overalls* although the standard overalls at that time were brown. Stranger still, although Goddard was zooming over them at an unusually low, and dangerous – indeed, prohibited – height, nobody seemed to notice him, or look up. He only just managed to clear the roof of the hangar. For that offence he could have been court-martialled.

Suddenly, he found himself out of the sunlit area and back in the turbulent conditions that had made him seek a landmark, but he gained height, battled on, and landed at Andover at eleven o'clock. In the officers' mess he described the extraordinary adventure to those present, who included Wing Commander A.C. Stevens and Wing Commander Haylock. Their natural response was to advise him to 'take more water with it' next time! A reputation for eccentricity, credulity or superstition does not advance one's prospects in a discplined Service, and thereafter Goddard kept quiet about his disturbing experience.

Later developments in the RAF proved beyond a shadow of doubt that he had flown from the present into the future – had witnessed in clarity and detail a scene not yet encompassed. For with the coming of the war, Drem airfield was rebuilt and reopened as a flying school, equipped with *yellow* Avro 504N biplanes and Magister monoplanes of the types he had seen in 1935. To the end of his days, Sir Victor Goddard (later Lord Goddard) had absolutely no doubt of the reality of precognition.

The manner in which certain disasters are sensed, if not actually foreseen, before they occur is very baffling, because disasters of all types are so numerous. In every country in the world, at any given moment, some human drama or tragedy is being enacted, some accident or disaster occurring.

Why should *some* of these be foreseen, and not others? If one were speaking merely of premonitions – those 'hunches' which so often prove well-founded – it would be no matter for surprise. So many millions of people have so many hunches that by a law of averages (or a commonsense assessment of what averages might reasonably be held to constitute a 'law') some proportion of those hunches must prove to be correct. But when it comes to strong convictions, or factual previsions, the whole problem is quite different. There have been shipwrecks aplenty, yet the sinking of the *Titanic* was undoubtedly seen (yes, seen) by quite a few people, including an informant of mine, before it occurred, and at a time when any misgivings as to that famous ship's seaworthiness would have been considered nonsensical.

Equally, there have been quite a few air disasters. Why are some foreseen and not others?

The fate of the giant airship R-101 which, in 1930, left Cardington at 7 p.m. on Saturday 5 October for India and crashed on a hill near Beauvais, France, at 2.05 a.m. killing all forty-six on board, including Lord Thomson, Minister for Air, and Air Vice-Marshal Sir Sefton Brancker, was foreseen by several people.

Forty-six of those on board were burned to death. A quarter of an hour before the crash those on board had no warning of any danger, although the airship had run into stormy weather. The French Air Ministry had radioed that the airship was within one kilometre from Beauvais, to which they had replied with a laconic 'Thank you'. Within minutes of that message the worst disaster in air history (at that time) occurred. Low-lying cloud prevented the R-101 from rising and the storm, by leaving masses of heavy rain on the top of the gas-filled envelope, forced the R-101 down until she struck a low hill by a wood near the village of Allonne. A few survivors owed their lives to the fact that water from burst water tanks swept them, protected from the tremendous heat, through the flames to safety.

I cannot prove, since I kept the information to myself at the time, that I had a distinct premotion of the R-101's fate as I watched it fly over London from the top of the *Daily Sketch* building, which was then in Gray's Inn Road off Holborn. While everybody gasped with amazement at the monster thundering slowly through the sky, I felt absolutely convinced that it would not make the journey to India – its intended destination. But, as I say, I kept my misgivings to myself, and when they proved justified, I had no means of proving, had I wished, that I had ever entertained them. In those days I was far too busy to keep a diary, a habit I cultivated later in life.

Eileen Garrett, however, had several distinct and specific precognitions of the R-101 disaster, and describes them in her memoirs, published shortly before her death (*Many Voices*, Allen & Unwin, 1969):

> The perceptions that I receive are clear-cut and distinct, like the unrolling of a film or spool. This is what living can be likened to: a continual unwinding of the thread from the spool – a current of feeling moving in space in the continuity of progress and unity of action ...
>
> The loss in 1930 of the airship known as the R-101 had been 'seen' by me three times in a period of five years. I know nothing about the mechanism of flying craft but, as I have mentioned, I did live in London during the Zeppelin raids in World War I. I had, like many thousands of people, watched their progress over London, watched the searchlights pick up their position, and seen them fall from the sky in flames. In fact, in company with young friends, I had hurried to the scene of one such disaster at Cuffley near Potters Bar, some thirty miles from London.
>
> I was specially troubled by these air raids, but my work demanded that I live in the heart of London. I was extremely worried for the safety of my child, then a baby. Finally I took her out of London to safety.
>
> I had, like others in London, learned to dread the nightly appearance of these ships; when I first saw this phantom zeppelin, many years had elapsed. My daughter had grown up and England was at peace. I have asked myself many times if my subconscious mind had made this image 'concrete' – but, if so, why was it projected in 1926, 1928 and 1929, and again in trance many times?
>
> The first appearance of the phantom airship occurred in Hyde Park. I had taken my terrier to the Serpentine to swim. I looked above, and there was a silver ship moving easily in the direction of the west. It made no conscious impression on me then. I had no relationship with anyone who might be flying. It was simply there in the sky. There

was no confusion, and it flew above me slowly to vanish into the sunset.

I saw the same object again two years later. I was in the neighbourhood of Holland Park en route to the College of Psychic Science. It was about 2 p.m. A high wind was blowing fleecy clouds across the sky. Out of a bank of clouds I saw an airship. It wobbled, then dipped. Puffs of smoke blew out and hid the undercarriage. Then the clouds covered it.

When I left the College I bought the late papers, expecting to read of the disaster. But there was nothing on the front pages, nor was there anything next day. This time I was confused. I had actually seen smoke, even as I had seen it happen during the 1916 raids. Through that week I watched the daily papers, but once again there was no account to be found.

I again saw the airship overhead in 1929, and again smoke emerged from the great envelope. I remember standing still frozen to the spot. White puffs caught the rays of the sun, then turned into a dense cloud. Again the clouds obscured the smoking ship. This time I was deeply upset. I knew this was serious. That it wasn't happening was unthinkable – but again there was no report.

After three such phantom happenings, it was hard to convince myself there had been no airship. Yet no one could explain it. There had been no known airship disaster anywhere. I often wondered why such visions happened to one so completely disinterested as I was.

Later, it was publicly announced that England was building two airships, the R-100 and the R-101. I began to meet people who were scheduled to fly to India, among them Sir Sefton Brancker, then head of the Air Ministry in London. I knew a friend whose home he was visiting one weekend, and I told her of the experience. When she related it to him he treated it laughingly. He did ask me 'Have you any idea which ship will suffer?'. 'The R-101' I replied. 'That's a help,' he said, 'That's the one scheduled to fly to India, and I am going on the journey soon.' Nothing more was said at the time.

Eileen Garrett's presetiments about the R-101 were true enough, but so were others. Captain Hinchcliffe, who lost his life flying the Atlantic, had sent many warning messages to his close friend, who was to become the navigator of the R-101. Mrs Hinchcliffe had been brought to a Spiritualist seance after her husband's death, and on receiving this message, made a special journey to Norfolk to warn her late husband's friend. Unfortunately, thought not surprisingly (since few serving men – if any – would refuse their duties because of a warning of this kind) the warning was ignored.

I am indebted to Edwin J.M. Holmyard, of Sandford Road, Winscombe, a retired engineer who, at the time of the R-101 affair, was working with some of the team who designed it in Bristol, for a new and interesting sidelight on this disaster.

Two days before it happened a colleague of Mr Holmyard's, with whom he was working, came in with a story of a terrifying nightmare which his wife had had, in which she believed herself trapped in a burning airship. 'The vivid details impressed me,' Mr Holmyard told me, 'the more so because I knew the scene near Beauvais and had many times spoken to Sir Sefton Brancker, who was one of the victims. Mrs Bond, who had this awful dream before the event, did not know anybody connected directly with this project. At the time the story was related it was the subject of much ribald comment – until the dream proved prophetic. It was a particular shock to me, because doing liaison work at Dunkirque between Headquarters, RNAS and Army groups, at the time of the formation of the Royal Air Force, I spoke to General Sir Sefton Brancker everyday'. Although now eighty-one years old, Mr Holmyard's memory is absolutely clear and he remembers vividly every detail of the tragic affair.

The number of people who foresee, correctly, that a plane flight is to end in disaster is larger than one would generally suppose. It could be argued that, with aviation now a part of our daily lives, and thousands of planes getting airborne all over the world, all day and every day, there must be a less hardy minority who view the hazards of flying with more trepidation than the rest. In the very nature of flying, it can never be regarded as wholly safe. Weather hazards, the fallibility of human nature both as

regards pilots and the servicing of aircraft, the machin-
ations of the deranged and the merely conspiratorial –
hijackers, political fanatics and the like – and, of course,
the fallibility of machines and their innumerable parts,
imply *some* risk, however minimal. Gravity is the aircraft's
biggest enemy. If something goes wrong it cannot pull
into a siding, like a car that has burst a tyre. One can
argue, then, that some people will always be apprehensive
and that by some unassessed 'law of average' some of
these apprehensions will be confirmed by events.

Personally, I am not sure it is as simple as that. Other
aviators besides Sheila Scott have claimed that the senses
are heightened by flying. Perhaps certain receptivities, or
atavistic capacities usually dormant because of the
numerous demands and distractions of sophisticated life,
are reactivated by flying in the air. Many air staff have
remarked upon the fact that second sight seems to be
developed after much experience of air travel. One BOAC
air hostess, Rosalind Unwin, remarked after the Heathrow
air disaster of April 1968, 'After a while crew members get
a sort of second sight.' She herself had had an intuition of
the crash, and so, too, did one of the surviving passengers,
Roberta Burke. When visiting her sister before the flight,
she had said that she was sure something terrible was
going to happen. The conviction did not, however, induce
her to postpone the flight.

Some passengers, however, follow their hunches on
these occasions. An Indian princess, the Maharanee of
Chota Undepur, owes her life to the fact that her secretary
had such a strong premonition of disaster when her
mistress was about to emplane at New Delhi on an Indian
Dakota that the Maharanee cancelled her seat. The plane
crashed shortly after leaving, and all its eighteen
passengers were killed.

In 1972 a last-minute change saved the lives of one
German couple, who were due to fly from Tenerife in the
Canary Islands. Frau Hildegarde Artmeier who, with her
husband, was actually on the Spanish-owned Corvair
airliner Coronado prior to take-off, *insisted* that they leave
the plane at once and travel with a second group of

tourists aboard a BAC 1-11 of the West German line Bavaria. The Spanish-owned plane crashed as it took off from the holiday airport. The victims included 143 Germans, three Austrians and two Italians. All of the party were owners or employees of travel firms in Bavaria. Why did Frau Artmeier insist at the last minute on changing planes? Considerations of comfort or time had absolutely nothing to do with it, there were no variations of service or attention and no reason whatsoever to suppose that anything would go amiss. But she was right. How did she know that the *second* plane would not crash, but the first would? As it was, the Coronado took off, rose to about sixty feet and then plummetted to the ground and burst into flames at the end of the runway. A strong conviction of impending disaster affects only those who feel it, the decision whether or not to act upon it is, of course, a purely personal one.

Whether a 'clearing house' for forecasts and precognition would ever be socially useful is a far more debatable matter. There was some such talk at the time of the foundation of the British Premonitions Registry, of the eventual possibility of some unspecified type of 'early warning system'. But the prior assessment of the value of precognitive forecasts would, it seems to me, be an almost impossible responsibility to discharge. One cannot imagine train schedules, flight schedules and public occasions being postponed or cancelled because of visual imagery, dreams or other seemingly precognitive glimpses, however vivid and convincing. It would dislocate public life and introduce a note of further anxiety and stress into a pattern of life which many already think too complicated. There would, too, be an inevitable harvest of hoax calls, cranky calls, and the apprehensions and fears of unstable or merely nervous people. Life was never meant to be lived in trembling anticipation of every step. Yet in this mass of material there could be certain warnings that time would justify, warnings which, if taken seriously and acted upon soon enough, might enable inspections, additional cautions and checks by which an otherwise inevitable disaster might be averted.

More will no doubt be discovered of the nature of precognition, and perhaps, even, some means of sorting the wheat from the chaff of the proffered predictions.

But even as it is, those who have precognitive convictions do not always get a dusty answer from the authorities. Quite often police authorities act, however reluctantly or sceptically, upon 'hunches' or 'visions' imparted to them by members of the public and, without encouraging a complicating traffic, have on occasions found some residues of useful truth.

Even aviation authorities do not turn a deaf ear, and will at least make enquiries, even if they do not by inference accept that the matter is as urgent as the enquirer feels. Two years ago, for example, an American who had a vivid dream of an aircraft crashing at Heathrow airport telephoned the airport to warn them. He was Sidney Simons, a 35-year-old translator of Upper Holloway. He clearly saw a plane crashing from the sky and heard the words 'Paris 743'. A machine-gun 'flashed into his mind' and he also heard a man's name.

He was so sure that there would be an accident that he telephoned Heathrow. The airport authorities told all airlines to check their flight records. Pan Am found that one of their Jumbos was 743 and was due to pass through Paris on its way from Frankfurt to New York. There were also 743 flights for TWA, Quantas and BEA but none of these were going to Paris.

In the event, nothing happened to confirm the forecast.

The strange story of Sir Victor Goddard seeing an airfield before it was rebuilt can be capped by a more recent story of a schoolgirl who saw a plane crash shortly *before* it happened:

The girl, Alison Nunn, aged ten, of Corstophine Hill Gardens, Edinburgh, was standing outside her home on 9 December 1970 with her sister Muriel, aged fourteen, when she saw a plane in trouble. Her sister saw it too. Smoke and flames were pouring from it and it must obviously crash at any minute. They raced inside the house to tell their mother, but by the time Mrs Nunn has listened to their breathless story and raced out to see what was happening, the plane had vanished.

*Two-and-a-half hours later* the Caledonian BAC 1-11 jet with seventy people on board had an engine flame-out as the plane took off from the airport. The flame-out was clearly visible from where Alison lived.

Why did she see it over two hours before it happened?

# 9   Winners, Treasure and Inventions

Can precognition play any part in the success of certain gamblers?

I am not talking of 'systems' – there are systems galore and one American professor, by using a computer, even devised a system that gave the advantage to the player, as distinct from the house, in crap games.

It is nearly twenty years ago now since I myself believed I had devised some means of increasing the probability of winning at football pools. The odds against winning a worthwhile prize on the pools are many millions to one, and, apart from that, the chances of knowing which quick brain and adroit foot will set a ball shooting between two posts at a far-distant match, would appear to be nil.

Nevertheless, by some type of concentration I not only began to win, but won eleven weeks in succession – a most unusual run which had not occurred before and has certainly never happened since. During that period, my thought was not, 'Have I won this week?' but 'how much have I won?'

By any criteria, a succession of eleven consecutive wins is curious and interesting, but the method, if it could be called a method, of my devising was not wholly or even consciously precognitive. Taking into account the 'track record' of the respective opponents in each match, purely in the statistical sense and with no regard to what is called form, I merely tried to imagine where the balance would lie.

At no point did I come near to achieving everyone's pipe-dream – the big win. No win was really large – in fact, the largest was forty-seven pounds and by the end of the run the wins had dwindled to shillings before they ended altogether and left me to face the harsh realities of economic life. Further, I had begun to find the process of concentration-cum-deduction tedious.

On the few occasions that I have played roulette – in places of so unlikely an assortment as Loew's Casino in Monte Carlo, the Berenice Hotel in Benghazi, in Libya, the Isle of Man Casino and the Playboy Club in London – I have had more than average luck and sometimes remarkable runs of 'single' number wins. Again and again, too, when I have not backed a number I fancied, it has come up. This foreknowledge, brief though it was, never operated if I was fatigued or preoccupied with other matters; it seems as though precognition, even of this brief duration, cannot operate when there is a seepage of nervous or mental energy.

It would be encouraging to think that precognition, whether spontaneous or by some means devised, can achieve some fortunate or happy and practical result. It has been observed, however, not without justice, that the majority of prophecies and predictions foreshadow gloom and doom. So far as spontaneous precognitive glimpses or 'mental gazes' are concerned, this cannot be avoided, but it would be only human to wish to avoid companions whose dire predictions not only depress and cause apprehension, but come true as well!

In 1972 one pools winner, a London bus conductor, Mr Steve Bammeke, a 38-year-old Nigerian then earning £25 a week, won £57,000 on Vernons Pools, thereby fulfilling a prediction of a gipsy fortune-teller who, three years previously, told him that he would win a fortune.

It happened on the sea front at Folkestone. The fortune-teller refused to take her customary fee of a guinea (twenty-one shillings then, or the equivalent of 105 pence nowadays) telling him: 'You can't afford to pay my guinea fee now, so I will give you a free reading, but one day you will come looking for me.' Strange to say, a local diviner in Nigeria had told him when he was eighteen that he would return to Nigeria bringing a lot of treasure.

A more dramatic example of precognition bringing

material gains is that of the late Dr John Williamson, a hard-up Canadian geologist who suddenly 'knew' that diamonds did not *have* to be found inside mountains. He had a strong mental vision that they could be found in a plateau, and saved up to go to what was then Tanganyika (the mainland area of Tanzania and former United Nations International Trust Territory under British Administration which became independent in 1961).

This was just before World War II. Most of his friends thought him crazy, but he got to Tanganyika, and selected the plateau of Shinyanga, where he dug for two years. This tireless prospecting got him nowhere, but in 1940 he found a diamond mine twenty miles from Shinyanga, and by the time he died eighteen years later he was known as the King of Diamonds. One in ten of the world's diamonds came from his mine, which in that time netted him a fortune of seven-and-a-half million pounds. He maintained – and who would disagree with him? – that his hunch had paid off.

However, John Williamson's good fortune was more a matter of courageously following a hunch, rather than gambling in the usual sense of that word. Nearer precognition was the experience of a Dutchman who in 1947 dreamed repeatedly of the number 3,684. He bought a ticket of that number with the Dutch state lottery and the number came up. Then there was the case of Joseph Almond of Hove, Sussex who won £221,616 in the football pools in 1966. Normally he only played a very small stake. Three weeks before he won he had a strong inclination to increase his stake to £1, thereby vastly increasing the number of lines in his permutation and, of course, his chances of winning. His larger stake entitled him to two hundred lines and the winning line was the 168th! If he had not acted on his premonition he would not have won.

Several informants have told me corroborated stories of having foreseen the results of races in what I can only describe as a kind of mental vision, although others report vivid and specific dreams that enabled them to place successful bets.

Harold Horwood, a retired chartered electrical engineer,

living in Cheshire, has for over thirty years had considerable success in this respect. Sometimes the information comes to him in dreams, at other times in what he describes as 'waking visions'. Charities have tangible proof of his success – he made his first donation to charity in 1946 from the proceeds of his winnings, and, more recently, gave £100 to the Institution of Electrical Engineers' Benevolent Fund in 1974.

In 1964 he dreamt the winners of a double and won £1,000 for a £5 stake. Since then he has had about seventy prophetic dreams, culminating in the recent Derby winner, Snow Night, which he backed at ante-post odds of 66-1.

Mr Horwood has his own views on the nature of precognition. 'It is now quite clear to me that some spirit entities have the faculty of seeing what to us is the future, and when they feel disposed, and when conditions are suitable, they are able to inform us mortals, by inducing dreams and/or by causing us to have waking visions. They are nowadays quite commonplace with me. They seldom spell out the name of the horse, but make me use my own intelligence to interpret the meaning'.

Obviously this unusual sort of contact seems real enough to Mr Horwood, and certainly the results are tangible – there is absolutely no question about that, as his bookmakers know well enough. Mr Horwood specifies the race in which he is interested. 'My interpretation', he tells me, 'is not always correct, and sometimes the indications are vague. In these cases I do not bet a big sum (neither do I when it is clear – but more than otherwise). I won two hundred and seventy pounds on a recent Derby at fifty to one. My recent improvement in these precognitions I put down to the fact that I swear to use *all* my winnings unselfishly.'

There is about Mr Horwood an engaging sincerity, and there is absolutely no question that, irrespective of the true sources of this strangely accurate intuition, he is ahead of most people in the number and accuracy of his precognitive glimpses.

A rather curious, and appropriate, dream brought

gambling success to Mr E.G. Dackombe, of Hainault, Essex:

> This happened the year the racehorse Airborne won the Derby. The night before the race I dreamt that I was sleeping in an upstairs bedroom. I was looking out of the window and I could see a horse jumping up to the bedroom window, it was up in the air! Next morning this made me curious, so I looked in the newspaper to see what horses were running. I found 'Airborne' was one of them. Not being a gambler, I nevertheless asked my father (a regular backer of horses) to put a bob each way on Airborne, which romped home to win me 66 to 1, £3 for my two shillings.

Mr Dackombe recalls his father's disgruntled comments about one-a-year punters 'spending out a couple of bob and winning'. He has sometimes repeated the experiences, and noticed that his precognitive glimpses are usually successful after he has helped somebody financially. A sort of psychic quid pro quo.

An equally curious 'lead' to a winning horse occurred to Mr Charles Agates, of Lawson Road, Colwyn Bay, North Wales. He began to have dreams about horses from 1936 onwards – about horses, not merely or exclusively about horse-*racing*. Thus, in one dream, he was watching a farmer trying to get his two horses to pull a load of straw out of his yard. He was whipping them, but it did no good, so he went into the house and sat on a chair with his head in his hands. Four days later, Mr Agates was in his shop when he suddenly heard a terrible rumbling outside on the road. Looking out, he saw a dray being drawn by two horses, which had galloped away without their driver. Mr Agates ran after them and stopped them.

His next experience was in a dream. He dreamt that he was 'shouting out along the street, in the gutter, COTTENEASTER. Next day a horse called Cottoneaster won at Kempton Park Jubilee at 100 to 9.'

Some time later Mr Agates envisaged the death of a friend in a dream. He told me:

My next experience concerned a horse. I was sitting in a chair by the fireside and dozed. During that time I seemed to be talking to a Brigadier General. Well, this General was saying to me that he had won all the battles he had been in. On the following day I was looking down the names of the horses, and beside one of them I wrote the comment *Cert*. This horse was called *Brigadier General*. My friend saw me write *Cert* beside the name and said 'How do you know?' The horse had never been seen before. I said, 'Don't worry, he will win, and all his races'. Sure enough, the horse won at 100 to 8. Also he won every race afterwards.

Another corroborated account of precognition used as an aid to successful gambling was given to me by Mrs Celia Hewett, of Hartley, in Kent. Because of what seemed to her friends and parents to be psychic propensities – a high degree of intuitive and interpretative capacity – she had been told that she would make a 'good medium'. Certainly she found herself at an early age 'knowing' which horses would win particular races; this information came to her in vivid dreams, which were in colour, and specific – void of all vagueness. I have a list, a considerable one, of her successful horse-racing forecasts, many of them at considerable odds (e.g. Pearl Diver, 40 to 1; Rockavon, 66 to 1; Sheila's Cottage, 50 to 1 and so on).

Mrs Hewett has become so accustomed to making these forecasts – which have benefited both herself and her friends financially – that she no longer bothers to keep records, but those she did elect to keep are certainly impressive, and her success continues.

Sometimes newspaper headlines are anticipated in dreams or visions (J.W. Dunne gives many instances of this) and this happens occasionally with racing results. Why it should do so is entirely beyond me and everyone else, but that it happens cannot be disputed and is a matter of proof. Miss Molly Aarstad, a retired advertising executive, of Oakfield Terrace, Gosforth, experienced precognition in many forms in her twenties and early thirties and was, in fact, in the habit of recounting her dreams to her mother at the breakfast table. Her brother, an admirer of J.W. Dunne, suggested that she follow his example by keeping a record of her dreams. Some of these were alarming, others ridiculous – yet they would come true. Once a nightmare was relived as she found herself alone, in utter darkness, at the foot of four flights of stairs and a burglar in the cellar behind her – this reproduced faithfully a dream she had experienced, and related, six weeks earlier. Then there was the curious dream in which she saw herself writing the words: *'I wonder whoever wants shoes for two left feet!'* By parcel post the next day some shoes her mother had ordered from London arrived. The parcel contained shoes for *two left feet*!

So far as horse-racing is concerned, Mrs Aarstad's information came by seeing newsprint in her dream. The paper gave the results of the Derby (yet, of course, to be run) and she clearly saw the name of Coronach first, Colorado second and a blurred third name. The early editions of the *Newcastle Chronicle* gave the results as she had seen them, the blurred name being Lancegaye.

Mr Donovan Massey, of Barlaston, Stoke-on-Trent, received his racing 'tips' in even more bizarre fashion:

> The remarkable one I will recount. It was about 1921. I was recently back from four years in the army, two-and-a-half years on the Western Front. I had no interest in horse-racing. I had never been on a race-course. One night I dreamed, and in my dream I was on a racehorse, and a horse was being led in by a tall lady. The scene shut off, to be replaced by another. In this, still on the racecourse, was a trestle table, on which was a huge cup. Several men (stewards) were on one side of the table and on the other, the tall lady who had led the horse in.
>
> At this stage a voice whispered in my ear, 'That is the Chester Cup'.
>
> The dream was so vivid that at breakfast I asked my Dad who was a regular punter, what was in the Chester Cup. He replied: 'The entries are not out yet. There is an acceptance stage later on, about April, the race being in May.' I told of my dream, which my Dad dismissed. I also told many others, who discounted its value. Later, I found that two ladies had entries in the race. Not too bad! At the acceptance stage, one of these was withdrawn. The other,

Mrs Soper Whitburn's horse, Chivalrous, proceeded to run and win the cup for the second year in succession at a starting price of seven to one. I backed my first horse, and won.

Much later, Mr Massey was sleeping in his bedroom, the walls of which were colour-washed in green. He found himself in a dream: watching a mysterious hand writing with chalk on the green wall 'DUCKS AND DRAKES'. It proved to be a horse with which Sir Edward Hulton won a big race at Manchester.

Mrs Ivy Henderson, a Chelsea housewife, receives her information about winners-to-be in a most unusual form. A sort of playlet is enacted within her dreams, followed by some type of display which registers in her memory when in a state of complete wakefulness.

I will merely instance two occasions. Some years ago, while sitting in the kitchen, she saw 'in mental gaze' a document signed by Capability Brown, (the famous eighteenth-century landscape gardener). The document was divided into several sections, which in full consciousness she noted and awaited the results at Newmarket. Thus she foresaw the winners of six races. In the sixth, incidentally, Capability Brown walked away with the race.

On another occasion, in a very curious dream, she saw a rostrum set up in a field, besides which jockeys were lined up. A magician – stage-type – mounted the rostrum. Doug Smith, one jockey, was on one side and Gordon Richards on the other. The magician tapped his black box three times with a black stick, then pulled out a straw boater, which he broke in two, handing Doug Smith one half and Gordon Richards the other.

Two weeks later, at Haydock Park, Mrs Henderson noticed that the first six races included both these jockeys. As printed in the paper, Doug Smith won the 'top half' of the two lists and Gordon Richards the bottom.

Like some others who foresee race results, she has experienced more dramatic and less pleasant glimpses of the future. One she describes as 'terrible'.

My father died in 1940. At the stroke of six o'clock on
Thursday 20 April 1973 he stood in the doorway of our
bedroom. I was so startled to see him I shot bolt upright
and asked what he wanted. Although he never spoke, I
knew he had come for my mother. I told my sister that
Mother would be going next Thursday. She thought me
mad. Mother died a day earlier than that – on Wednesday
26 April.

Miss Judy Cousins, an artist, of Earlsdon, Coventry,
finding that she had experienced several instances of
foreknowledge, tried a year or so ago to develop the
faculty and apply it at will. It grew from her short-lived
interest in horse-racing from 1948 to 1951.

> About 1961, after I had been discussing my 'theme' that the
> way to make money was simply to 'read' tomorrow's
> papers today, I was told to get on with it and 'read' the
> Derby winner in this way. This was at lunch, and having
> suggested quiet, I shut my eyes and concentrated on the
> next day's racing headlines. I remember reading a long and
> previously unknown name. On checking, this turned out
> to be a runner. It came in third at 100 to 1, thus, being
> backed each way, proving the best bet on the race.
>    Three months later, while I was working with an
> assistant in my studio, the radio went over to a
> commentary on a race of no particular importance. My
> assistant, who had heard about the previous incident said,
> out of the blue, 'Well, read this one'. There were very many
> runners and the last one mentioned was *Parthenon*. It was a
> neck and neck race but Parthenon won it at 20 to 1'.

Miss Cousins backs her hunches, and won comfortably on
these races. On one occasion all she could get was
'Goodfellow' which was not the name of a horse, but of a
*Daily Mail* tipster whose advice she once followed. So she
bought a copy of the paper, studied Goodfellow's tips for
the day and backed those. They won.

In her experience, too much conscious effort inhibits the
ability to precognize.

Something similar, I imagine, was discovered by Al
Koran (a pseudonym), a 'mind reader' who wrote out his

The marriage of Lord Dowding, British Air Marshal and head of Fighter Command, was foreseen by his future wife long before they had ever met. Lady Dowding has experienced many spectacular instances of precognition

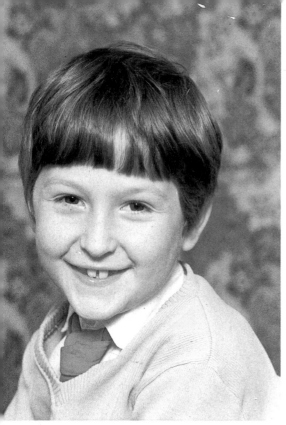

Paul Czarnecki, the happy
healthy boy who forecast his
own death

*Opposite*: George
Adamson, husband of Joy
Adamson, the author of
*Born Free*, was visited by
fifteen lions on the night
before his murder in 1989.
The author believes they
acted on a precognition of
his death

Mrs Stan Czarnecki with her
son's toy panda

Mrs Lorna Middleton (left), pictured with a friend. She was the music teacher and impresario who had a clear prevision of the Aberfan disaster of 1966 which was substantiated by Dr J.C. Barker, a distinguished psychiatrist and psychic researcher

Before the terrible disaster at Aberfan, Wales, in 1966 when an immense slag heap slid down the mountainside killing 144 people, 128 of which were children, several people had a clear precognition of the calamity. One of these was a 9-year-old pupil, Eryl Mai

Longleat, palatial home of the 6th Marquess of Bath, is one of Britain's great Elizabethan mansions, begun in 1568. The home of two ghosts, it was also the scene of a weird trick of time; the Marquess's mother found herself projected into the future

Portrait of the 5th Marchioness of Bath, mother of the present Lord Bath, who possessed many psychic gifts

President Lincoln (1809-65) dreamed three times – and in detail – that he would be assassinated. His assassination was predicted by the psychic William Douglas Home in 1863

The ill-fated *Titanic*, the White Star liner and the largest vessel of her time, as she appeared before her maiden voyage to New York, during which she sank with a loss of over a thousand lives. A vivid prevision of the disaster was seen by an informant of the author's, whilst under an anaesthetic

Mrs Valerie Goodsell whose
psychic experiences include
cases of precognition

Michael Bentine, the famous
television comedian, had a clear
precognition of his son's death
in a plane crash

COMMANDANT FELIX

John William Dunne (left) 1875-1949, philosopher, scientist and brilliant engineer, believed that precognition was scientifically proveable. His theories caused a worldwide sensation

This Dunne aircraft looks too frail to fly, but, like its prototypes, proved invaluable for reconnaissance. At this early stage in his life, Dunne was convinced, by his analysis of his dreams, that the future could be foreseen and that precognition was a fact

THE NEW DUNNE MACHINE.

J.W. Dunne's designs for the first British military aircraft, produced in the greatest secrecy before World War I, were widely used in the Royal Flying Corps.

forecast of the first three in the Two Thousand Guineas race of 19 April 1954, when he appeared in the television version of 'What's My Line?' He wrote his forecast on a £5 note, which was sealed, signed by the panel, and put into a bottle, which was also sealed. Later in another programme, 'Quite Contrary' the forecast was read out: '1. Darius; 2. Ferriol; 3. Arabian Night'. The first two were correct and Arabian Night was beaten for third place by Poona in a photo-finish. He did not back his own forecasts although the Chairman, Eamonn Andrews, did. 'Al Koran' incidentally, correctly forecast the results of the General Election in 1951.

In another connection, and not strictly germane to the central theme of gambling, except that the principal character was an enthusiastic sportsman, known on every racetrack in Britain, the following experience is certainly interesting:

Mr Neville Harper and his wife Margaret were sitting in the National Hotel, Ismaelia in north-eastern Egypt, at about seven o'clock in the evening. Mr Harper was serving with the Royal Air Force at the time. He informs me:

> For some reason or another, she made a comment about Tom Walls, a well known stage and film actor of that period. I replied: 'That can't be true because he is dead, I clearly remember reading about it in the paper. As a matter of fact, it was stated at the bottom of the column that he was very interested in horses and maintained a stable in Ireland'. My wife was rather puzzled and let the matter drop.
>
> Next morning I picked up the *Egyptian Gazette* and saw on the front page an article about Tom Walls. It stated that he had died in the earlier part of the previous evening. At the bottom of the column a comment was made to the effect that he was interested in horses and maintained a stable in Ireland.

Mr Harper now lives and works in Hayes, Middlesex, as a lecturer. Mrs Harper's recollecton of this puzzling incident is as detailed and emphatic as her husband's. She confirms his story in every respect. Both thought it weird that he should have 'read' a newspaper before it was printed!

Apart from gambling, and the success or near-misses of professional 'seers' who cater profitably for mere superstition or that vast army of people, outwardly self-reliant, who want their hands held in a psychological sense, are there cases of precognition achieving other useful or profitable purposes?

The picturesque market-town of Swaffham, in the eastern counties of England, is connected historically with an outstanding case of precognition. Indeed, the north aisle of Swaffham's church, which has an eighteenth-century spire and a sixteenth-century tower, was the gift of John Chapman, a fourteenth-century tinker who is depicted in Swaffham's crest.

Three times John Chapman had a dream in which it was impressed upon him that he should go to London Bridge, where he would meet a man who would make him rich.

Hundreds of years ago there were two simple choices of transport – your horse or your feet. John Chapman, the tinker-pedlar, was a very long way from London. People who roamed far from their own familiar localities did so at their own risk – of being robbed or murdered in the course of their journey, or becoming destitute for want of work and being designated a 'vagabond'. There were some fairly vicious laws against vagabonds, who were often flogged at the cart-tail.

Only the insistence of the dream, and its vividness and specific message, gave Chapman the courage to essay the lonely and uncomfortable journey, in the course of which his meagre resources were indeed exhausted, leaving him tired and hungry by the time he finally reached London Bridge.

Poor John Chapman walked up and down the bridge all day, looking at the motley throng that hurried each way, all intent on their affairs. Nobody knew him. Nobody sought to return his gaze or acknowledge him in any way. He was beginning to think he had been very foolish to leave his home on such a vague fool's errand, and was dreading the long and uncertain journey home again, which he would certainly have to make at any moment, when a stranger approached. The stranger observed that he had noticed John Chapman hanging about for a long time, and watched his movements with curiosity. What was he up to? Why was he staring and inspecting everyone who passed, and what brought him to London Bridge?

Chapman told him his dream. He explained how he had been instructed to come to London Bridge, where he would meet a man who would make him rich. The stranger replied that he thought it a preposterous speculation to act upon such a dream; why, he himself had experienced a most peculiar, an utterly absurd dream himself, which he had dismissed as so much nonsense. In *his* dream, he had been told to take himself off with all haste to a town called Swaffham, of which he had never heard, but which on enquiry he gathered was somewhere in distant Norfolk, and that in Swaffham there lived a tinker called John Chapman. There was a garden attached to the tinker's humble home, a garden that boasted only a single tree. Underneath that tree was buried a crock of gold.

One can imagine Chapman's surprise. With commendable self-control, however, he dissembled it. He did not reveal his identity. The amazing coincidence of the two dreams impressed him and convinced him that there could be 'something in it'. In any case, if he took himself off home, it would be easy to find out.

In due course he arrived back in Swaffham and, pausing neither to eat nor rest, began to dig under the tree. His spade struck a buried jar, which proved to be full to the brim with gold pieces. Furthermore, it bore a note: 'Dig deeper. Under me doth lie one rich than I'. Needing no pressing in the matter, John Chapman dug with great energy and found, sure enough, a second pot full of gold coins. He had uncovered a fortune. He proved, as I say, no greedy man, and used some of his treasure to benefit his own town, including his gift of an aisle to the church, which stands today as a monument to his generosity and his unusually good luck. His precognition came to him in an extraordinary way, but it proved true.

Useful information, leading to the discovery of documents vital to a claim on an estate, was once imparted to a Spanish family, according to Dr Cesar Camargo in his *Psycho-analysis of the Prophetic Dream* (Madrid, 1929; *Psicoanalisis del sueno profetico*).

A married couple, and their servant Antonia, were living in Caxorla. The husband's father had died recently, at his house in Jaen, and they were in mourning for him. Documents which would establish their entitlement under the will could not be found, and there were the inevitable family disputes as rival claims were pressed.

One night the servant was awakened from her sleep to observe the shadowy figure of a man standing at the foot of her bed, wearing a morning coat, top hat and white trousers. He said: 'Do not be afraid, girl. I am not going to do you any harm. Tell your master, my son, that the missing document is under the ninth tile, on the right as you go in, in the drawing-room in the house in Jaen'. The vision then disappeared and the girl fainted.

When she recovered, she made for her employers' bedroom, awakened them and told them what had happened. Terrified as she was, her story was coherent and specific. In particular she was asked to describe the figure she had seen most carefully, and it corresponded exactly with the appearance in life of the dead man. It was particularly significant, because the servant had only recently come to work for the couple and had never met the father.

The next morning her employer, described in the account merely as Mr N., went to his father's house in Jaen and there, under the ninth tile as he went in, and which he found to be loose, he found the missing document.

On the face of it, this looks like precognition. By the roundabout means of a servant's hallucination, they were led to the site of a badly needed document. However, Father Pedro Meseguer of the Society of Jesuits, a Spanish priest with a deep knowledge of psychology and parapsychology, in his careful and objective study, *The Secret of Dreams* (Burns and Oates, 1960) points out that, like so many paranormal phenomena, many interpretations of this occurrence are possible. Mr N. may have once been told, and meanwhile forgotten, the place where his father had placed the document for safe keeping. Although forgotten in his conscious mind, the information could still lie dormant in his subconscious, and he might in sleep even have visualized his father. By means of telepathy, both vision and information might have been picked up by the servant sleeping nearby. However, the explanation is at best a hypothesis. What is certain is that there was foreknowledge of the whereabouts of a missing document.

There is the equally remarkable, and absolutely authentic, story, of how the formula for benzene first came to Friedrich August von Kekule, Professor of Chemistry at Ghent, in 1865. For a long time he had tried to devise the atomic or molecular structure of benzene or, to give it its full description, trimethyl benzene.

He had turned his chair to the fire and dozed. It seemed that the atoms were dancing about before his eyes:

> ...the smaller groups kept modestly in the background. My mental eye, rendered more acute by repeated visions of this kind, could not distinguish larger structures, of manifold conformation; long rows, sometimes more closely fitted together; all twining and twisting in snakelike motion. But look. What was that? One of the snakes had seized hold of its own tail and the form whirled mockingly before my eyes. As if by a flash of lightning, I awoke.

The snake swallowing its tail had provided the vital clue – what was to constitute the ring-theory of the constitution of benzene.

The discovery was an epoch-making one for organic chemistry.

In a sense, this was a precognition of what he was to discover. There are examples, however, of precognition of what was yet to be created. I suppose those interested in hypnotism, psychology and sleep, with its various levels of consciousness or unconsciousness, might argue that from these levels information manifests itself which otherwise might have remained dormant, but that the information was there, in the mind, all the time. This I find a very facile theory, full of pot-holes.

The very word 'level' as applied to consciousness is hypothetical. That there are various strata, for want of a better word, I would not deny; otherwise, how account for the hypnotized subject, regressed by the operator into more and more distant days of the past, actually writing on a blackboard with the uncertain delineation of a schoolchild, complete with inadequate spelling? How account otherwise for the retrieval of detailed information which is not in the *conscious* mind at all? That the brain (and even more the mind, an abstract term symbolizing something equally abstract) retains far more information, both acquired, observed and instinctive than we can ever imagine, is an established fact. In experiments by which sections of the brain of a living person have been touched by gold antennae implanted through the skull, the subject had heard an entire symphony, heard only once years ago and long since 'forgotten'.

One of the most beautiful of eighteenth-century sonatas was first heard in a dream by its composer, Guiseppe Tartini (1692-1770). Born in Parano, the son of a wealthy Italian nobleman, he was intended either for the Church, for the Law, or for the Army and studied diligently for all these. He was an expert fencer and a violinist and composer of consummate skill.

His life was, like Cellini's in another period, a mixture of the hectic and the contemplative, the active and the creative. Having secretly married and been pursued by an angry cardinal, he took refuge in a monastery at Assisi, there conceiving and evolving the peculiar musical technique known today as 'Tartini's tone'. He also developed improvements to the violin itself.

The background to a sonata which he had written at the age of twenty-one was first heard by him in a fantastic dream, details of which he confided to the French astronomer, Joseph Jerome de Lalande (1732-1807), who, fortunately, noted the details of Tartini's weird account in his journals at the time.

Tartini dreamed that he had sold his soul to the devil. He seems, for a devout man, to have been completely at ease in the devil's company and, indeed, handed him his violin to see if he could play it! 'What was my astonishment,' Tartini declared, 'when I heard him play with a consummate skill a sonata of such exquisite beauty that it surpassed the audacious dreams of my imagination. I was delighted, transported, enchanted. I was breathless, and I woke up. Seizing my violin, I tried to reproduce the sound I had heard. But in vain. The piece I composed, *The Devil's Trill*, was the best I had written, but how remote it was from the one in my dream!'

The diabolically inspired creation (if indeed a conventional devil had a hand in it) marked a turning-point in Tartini's fortunes. Once, when he was playing the violin at a church service – at which his enemy the Cardinal was present – he was concealed from view behind a curtain. But a careless priest pulled aside the curtain, revealing him as the man behind the divine airs that gave lift and ethereal beauty to the more sonorous organ accompaniment. The Cardinal forgave him, his return was welcomed, and for thirty years thereafter he played pieces regularly in the famous church of Saint Anthony in Padua.

Tartini 'heard' *The Devil's Trill* played in his dream, and even 'saw' the long-tailed, web-winged king of darkness playing it. In so far as it presaged to a great degree what he subsequently committed to paper, it can be held to be precognition of a type. Again, one may talk of the uncharted shores of the subconscious mind. But what *is* the 'mind', as distinct from the brain and, even less easy to dogmatize about, the 'subconscious mind'? Those whom parapsychology and its mysteries merely exasperate have a habit of attributing far too many things to the workings of the subconscious mind. To do so is tantamount to 'explaining' a conundrum by means of a riddle.

Samuel Taylor Coleridge (1772-1834), son of the vicar of Ottery St Mary in Devon, who became one of England's greatest poets, conceived one of his best-known works, *Kubla Khan*, in a dream. At the time he was in poor health and for peace and quiet removed himself to a lonely

farmhouse near Lynton, a beautiful village whose pretty
stream is spanned by bridges, and which then was a mere
handful of small grey houses. He had been prescribed a
soporific or anodyne, and he fell asleep in his chair while
reading *Purchas's Pilgrimage* (more fully: 'Purchas his
Pilgrimage, or Relations of the World and the Religions
Observed in all Ages', published in 1613). He slipped into
sleep just as he was reading the sentence: 'Here the Khan
Kubla commanded a palace to be built, and a stately
garden thereunto. And thus ten miles of fertile ground
were enclosed with a wall'. Kubla Khan (1216-1294) was a
Mongol Emperor of China and grandson of Ghengis
Khan, to whose empire he succeeded in 1260.

Purchas's stories of great travellers are one of England's
most exciting literary treasures, and must have been
mental food indeed for Coleridge, who was otherwise in
low spirits.

It is, therefore, not surprising that with his lively
imagination and sensitivity, and in his drugged state, the
seed of the story he had been reading before he dozed off
bloomed in his imagination in new form. 'The author', it is
recorded, 'continued for about three hours in a profound
sleep, at least of the external senses, during which time he
has the most vivid confidence, that he could not have
composed less than from two to three hundred lines; if
that indeed can be called composition in which all the
images rose up before him as *things* without a parallel
production of the corresponding impressions, without
any sensations or consciousness of effort. On awakening,
he appeared to himself to have a distinct recollection of
the whole, and taking his pen, ink, and paper, instantly
and eagerly wrote down the lines here preserved'.

The 'series of images' he observed in his dream sound
like an enactment which, in his dream, became translated
into descriptive poetry. In this sense, again, it can fairly be
said that Coleridge had a preview of what was to become
an accomplished fact – a poem as often quoted as *The
Ancient Mariner*.

The astrologer, mathematician and philosopher, Jerome
Cardan, an Italian poet born in Paris (1501-1576), wrote his

most famous book, *De Subtilitate Rerum*, entirely as the result of a recurrent dream in which the whole form and content of the book was laid out before him. The dream persisted until he had completed his task – then it vanished, never to recur again.

A clearer case of precognition that brought benefits (albeit as a by-product of a tragedy) appears in a book, *The Anatomy of Sleep*, by a physician, Dr Edward Binns, published in 1845. My late friend and author, William Oliver Stevens of New York, mentioned it to me long ago in America, and quotes the story in a later work, *The Mystery of Dreams*.

The story is a good example of an event anticipated in detail – a totally unexpected event – as to be acceptable as an example of true precognition. William came across the story in the works of a worthy but neglected writer, Robert Dale Owen. When Owen discovered the account in Dr Binns' book, he set about verifying it in a businesslike manner. Unfortunately the central character had died, but his son, the Hon. Mr Talbot, was able to write out the story in fair detail. No doubt first-hand verification would have been better, but we can be thankful that, despite the lapse of time, Robert Dale Owen provided rather more verisimilitude than did Dr Binns.

The correspondent revealed that one night in 1768 his father, Matthew Talbot, of Castle Talbot, County Wexford, dreamed that he arose from sleep to find the atmosphere 'hazy':

> He went down into the library and seated himself at the desk, where he began writing. Then happening to look up and out of the window, he saw at the end of a long avenue of trees a horseman approaching the house. The man wore a blue jacket and was riding a white horse.
>
> Talbot, in the dream, rose from the desk and went to the window, which he opened, and looked out. The stranger rode up to the window and handed Talbot a roll of documents. He explained that these were ship's papers, invoices of the cargo of a vessel which had been wrecked off the coast and had drifted in upon the shore of the near-by estate of Talbot's son-in-law, Lord Mount Morris.

As he looked at the papers, Talbot saw that they were signed 'Bell and Stephenson'. That was all. But he dreamed the same little scene, identical in every circumstance, *three times that night*. This was so extraordinary that he told his wife about it in the morning.

Then he rose, dressed and went down stairs, noticing as he glanced outside that the air was misty. He seated himself at his desk in the library – apparently as his regular custom. Something made him look up and out of the window. There, at the end of the tree-lined vista, he saw a horseman coming, the identical man he had seen in his dreams. He wore a blue jacket but he rode a grey horse. Talbot opened the window. Up rode the stranger, saying that he came from Lord Mount Morris. He produced a roll of papers, explaining as he did so that they were the invoices taken from the wreck of an American vessel which had drifted in upon his lordship's estate. He added that there was no person left on the wreck to lay claim to what remained of ship or cargo. His lordship felt that his father-in-law had better have the documents in his possession. The only means of identification of these papers was the signature 'Stephenson and Bell'.

'I can assure you,' wrote the Hon. Mr Talbot to Robert Dale Owen, 'my dear sir, that the above actually occurred and is most faithfully given.'

This is an extraordinary case of precognition, in which there are few deviations from dream to reality. The white horse of the dream proved to be grey, and the name on the documents was reversed. Otherwise every detail transpired as in the dream. By a matter of several hours, Matthew Talbot saw something which had not yet happened. It was not something that had ever happened to him before. It was not something which could be assumed to be likely to happen by virtue of anything in his family's history. Nor had anything transpired at the time to make it reasonable to anticipate anything of the kind. Time had played tricks with him. The effect had come before the cause.

# 10   Crimes Previewed

A few years ago a smartly dressed, middle-aged man walked into Wallington police station.

The sergeant-in-charge came over politely.

'Can I help you, sir?'

'Well,' said the caller, 'I don't really know whether you can or can't – I just felt I should look in ...'

'Yes.'

'I've got a rather peculiar story to tell you. I had a strange vision last night ...'

'Oh yes, sir', said the sergeant, doing his best to look as though what he was to hear was to prove of absorbing interest. 'What was it?'

The caller explained: 'Two little girls were murdered in Sunderland, and I had this strange vision of them, and they appear to be the same people in the newspaper, the following day ...'

'Well, sir,' the sergeant replied, 'I suggest you get in contact with the Sunderland police.'

The caller was disappointed, and a trifle exasperated. He had information which he *thought* might have some relevance to the crime, and he was merely being invited to make trunk calls at his own expense to a far-distant police station.

'If that's what it's going to be like, forget it.' He started to leave.

'Excuse me, sir,' said the sergeant, politely, 'I must take your name and address.'

Having given them, the caller left. But it was not long before his telephone was ringing and the police were asking to come and see him. They had themselves contacted the Sunderland police, and they would like to hear more of his 'vision', as he put it.

In the event, they questioned him for nearly two hours and wanted, naturally enough, to know where he was on the night of the crime.

What was the vision of which the caller spoke? I went to see this caller, whose name does not, I think, add any special relevance or interest to this particular account, and his experience was very strange indeed.

He had his vision on 17 July 1973:

> I awoke at about three o'clock in the morning with a strange vision which was very, very real. I saw two little girls – one with bobbed hair, one with longer hair; one was lying on the floor, unconscious as it seemed to me, and the other was being strangled in a strange way on a table top. There was a light burning above a deal table, very much as if it was in a shed. It was so real – I was standing at the side of the man. I could see his profile. He was youngish, but it's hard to say his actual age. He seemed to have had a brain storm because he was saying to himself that what he didn't want to do was to have to kill the second girl. This was very, very real. The following morning I looked at the newspaper and found that two little girls had been murdered in Sunderland. The photograph was of the girl I had seen being strangled.

I asked him more about his vision. Where was he? He was in bed with his wife. *How* did he see it – in 'mental gaze' as Churchill used to say? No. It seemed real, as though he was actually standing at the man's side while he was committing the crime.

I asked: 'Presumably you came out of this vision, so to speak?'

He told me: 'I was awake whilst it occurred. It was very much like a pre-play – awakening from a dream when you see the whole thing in front of you. It was very real, but not frightening, strangely enough.'

'Was the vision in monochrome or colour?'

'In colour.'

'Was it flat or stereoscopic?'

'Stereoscopic' (i.e. solid-looking, three-dimensional, with a sense of 'depth' and perspective).

There were many points of correspondence between what this man 'saw' and what transpired. What was remarkable was that a vision so definite should have occurred.

In recent years parapsychology, as the spectrum of unexplained phenomena is broadly described, has become increasingly recognized in academic and official circles as containing some nucleus of hard fact, and of having some potential usefulness. The difficulty of defining certain phenomena satisfactorily, or of producing them to order so that their nature can be examined and measured in acceptable scientific terms and standards, naturally imposes limitations and inhibitions on the authorities who are thus approached. Such terms as 'clairvoyant', 'psychic' and so on are easily enough assumed, and there are few, if any, criteria by which authorities can measure credibility. Even so, they are far more disposed to listen to, and follow up, psychic or precognitive leads than they were years ago. Ridicule has been replaced by cautious interest, and in some cases by a 'it-can't-hurt-to-try' attitude. This is particularly true of crime, the fighting of which is and will always be a severely practical business.

Cicero (106-43 BC) describes how two youths who journeyed to Megara stayed there in different places, one at an inn and the other with friends. The latter *saw* his friend appear in distress to say that the landlord of the inn was plotting to murder him. He later appeared again, this time to say he was dead, and that his body was to be smuggled through the city gates concealed in a dung-cart. Thus warned, the friend waited at the gates for the dung-cart to appear, and, halting it in its course, found the body of his murdered friend. Cicero was a truthful and dependable historian. His account implies that the young man had a precognition of his friend's death – information of his murder *before* it came to pass.

In modern times, a friend of mine, the late Captain Dod Orsborne, had an equally alarming precognitive experience. I should say at once that Captain Orsborne, as all who knew him would cheerfully affirm, was not a man easily frightened. A hard-living, tough, wiry little man with piercing eyes and neatly trimmed beard, he was, I suppose, the modern equivalent of the pirate or merchant adventurer. As skipper of the *Girl Pat*, during the Spanish Civil War in the thirties, he had been in trouble gun-running for the Republicans, and that was only one episode in his adventure-packed life.

He told me that, while on a lonely watch in the North Sea a spectre of the second mate, who had not for some unexplained reason rejoined the ship, appeared to him. The experience was unnerving. He even heard the man, in his familiar voice say, 'Come and get me, Dod.'

Later, in his cabin, as Captain Orsborne was about to get some sleep, the figure of the second mate appeared again, again with the sad, frantic appeal, 'Come and get me, Dod.'

Later it was discovered that the second mate had been attacked and robbed as he was about to rejoin his ship, and had slipped into the water and been drowned. His body was discovered after the ship had left.

By an interesting irony, Captain Orsborne was himself the victim of similar violence, being attacked and murdered at the docks at Marseilles. When he told me his story, of the second mate, he was under the impression that the first vision came to him before his second mate was killed. If that were so, his experience could be classed as a combination of precognition and telepathy (as with the story related by Cicero) for, as I am always at pains to emphasize, so often one type of paranormal phenomenon merges with another.

A Dutch-born clairvoyant (some have described him as a 'mind-reader', a description which can only be accepted with reservations) was called in by the Boston police when they were hunting for the Boston Strangler. Many of the conclusions which Peter Hurkos reached were uncannily accurate and enabled the police (who had at first been extremely cynical about the mere possibility of his services being of any use to them in their enquiries) to narrow the field in their search. Some were amazed at the accuracy of some of his assertions.

Peter Knecht, a young and respectable lawyer, was a

friend of Jay Sebring, one of the victims in the Hollywood massacre in which Sharon Tate lost her life. He called Peter Hurkos to visit Roman Polanski's estate. The Los Angeles police were understandably somewhat bemused as Hurkos went through the house, examining dried bloodstains and giving his views on the circumstances of the killings. He did not, incidentally, tell them that a woman participated in the murders, as was subsequently established, but many of his prognostications proved correct. But, as I say, he was engaged in this instance by a lawyer and not by the police. As one policeman said at the time: 'If we resorted to calling him in officially we would probably be the laughing-stock of the entire police world. So officially we don't comment about him.'

However, Hurkos's involvement in these enquiries was not of the nature of *precognition*, which is knowledge of a future event and not the interpretation of a past event. Its relevance in this context is merely to make the point that, to some extent at least, the fact that an element of paranormal knowledge might be accepted in the pursuit of police enquiries is more likely than it was.

Even so, Peter Hurkos has experienced precognition and once foresaw the future so accurately that it made him an object of suspicion, a suspicion that nearly cost him his life. In his personal memoirs, *Psychic*, he describes how, when he was in the Zuidwal hospital in the Hague during the last war, he had a strong premonition (or rather, precognition, since his information was specific) about a fellow-patient.

Hurkos was very ill, having injured his skull in a thirty-foot fall. The patient, about to be discharged after an emergency appendectomy, came to say goodbye to him. Hurkos had the sudden conviction that the man was a British agent, and that he was going to be killed by the Germans in Kalverstaat in a few days time.

Even when a doctor came and enquired what the trouble was, Hurkos persisted in asking them to stop the man. But it was too late. Two days later, the British agent, who had been parachuted into Holland, was killed by the Gestapo on Kalverstaat.

Lest it be asked why, in the event, the Gestapo did not elect to arrest the man whilst he was in hospital, the answer seems to have been that the Gestapo had 'cracked' the codes being used at the time, and were informed about the proposed 'drops' of British agents in Holland. It would have been pointless to arrest them as they dropped; it was to their advantage to dissemble their knowledge and tail a suspect for a while, in the hope he would lead them to members of the Dutch underground movement.

This precognition had a most unwelcome sequel for Peter Hurkos. The agent having been killed, the Dutch resistance were naturally interested to hear that Peter Hurkos had revealed in advance the nature and place of the murder. How, they asked, could he have known? Their first and obvious assumption was that he must have been in collusion with the Gestapo (an unlikely thing really, for if he had been he would not have created such a scene in hospital, and attracted the attention of nurses, patients and doctors). At any rate, an execution squad arrived at his bedside in the hospital, and only by a dramatic last-minute demonstration that he could read his would-be executioner's thoughts was Hurkos saved.

In the tracing of missing people, precognition has on occasion played an important part. In fairly recent times, Gerard Croiset, another Dutch clairvoyant, has succeeded where the police have failed. He was called in to locate a boy who had been missing for twelve days. The psychic said that he was dead, described a weather vane and sent a sketch of the area to the police. He then drove to the Hague, visited a place which tallied with his description and to which (although the police did not tell him) police tracker dogs had already led them. Croiset confirmed that the boy had drowned there and predicted that the boy's body would surface in four days time about half a mile away. Although the police dragged the river at both places, without success, the boy's body did surface at the spot and at the time that Croiset predicted. It was not precognition, but clairvoyance, to know how the boy had died; but it was precognition to state accurately, in advance, when and where the body would be found.

An even more spectacular case of precognition, enabling a body to be found when every other effort to trace it had failed, was reported by Dr Paul Joire, Professor at the Psycho-Physical Institute of France, in *Psychical and Supernormal Phenomena* published in 1916. That it happened long ago in no way detracts from its interest or relevance, as the unknown principles that interest and mystify us have been an inherent part of life all along. One cannot suppose or believe that any principles (known or unknown) inherent in nature have suddenly become part of it. There have been cases of precognition since the dawn of recorded history. Period has nothing to do with the nature of the problem although, in the light of modern physics, and with scientific methods of eliminating the more obviously false hypothesis, we may examine modern precognitive phenomena in greater and more profitable detail.

The case concerns a Dr Harold Munch Peterson, of the Fredericks Hospital, Copenhagen, and son of a professor of medicine of that city. In October 1904, he came to Aix-les-Bains with a circular ticket *via* Germany and Switzerland, from where he should have proceeded to Paris by way of Lyons. He sent a postcard to his sister from Culos on 3 October, saying he was leaving for Aix, after which his family received no further news of him.

Dr Peterson had been carrying a letter of introduction to a Dr Cazalis, on whom he had not called.

The Prefecture of police in Paris had searched in vain for him. The Commissioner of police at Aix made enquiries and established that Dr Peterson did arrive at Aix, and on the morning of 5 October, before exploring the area on his bicycle, ordered eggs and tea for breakfast at his hotel and then left, saying that he would not return until the evening.

As he did not return at all, it was feared that he must have met with an accident on one of the surrounding mountains. The conscientious and enterprising Commissioner of police, M. Gauthier, who had traced Dr Peterson's arrival in Aix-les-Bains, also established that before leaving the hotel Dr Peterson had said that he intended going to Mont-du-Chat, which lies to the west of Aix-les-Bains and is one of the most dangerous of the mountains thereabouts. The police chief sent his men not only there but also to 'La Chabotte', a mountain 2,730 feet high which overlooks the eastern side of the lake. This area seemed all the more likely to produce a clue because Dr Peterson's two brothers, a doctor of law and a professor at Copenhagen University, had explored the area around the lake by car and several innkeepers said that they had seen a man corresponding to Dr Peterson's photograph riding around on a bicycle.

After exhaustive enquiries, and being still without a definite lead, the police received an anonymous letter:

Aix-les-Bains, October 26, 1904

To the Justices of the Peace.

Permit me to bring to your knowledge the following communication just received, and to remain anonymous for the present.

If by this means the body is discovered, I will make myself known by producing a copy of this letter.

The doctor died on a perpendicular precipice of the Revard, under an overhanging rock near a house which is used as a shelter for sheep when overtaken by storms. A point which will be very useful for discovering the body is to look for traces of blood on all the stones around the place in which it lies.

Further searches were made by gendarmes and foresters on the slopes of the Revard, and chalets searched, without success. Winter was coming on, and the paths would soon be covered in snow. The search was abandoned until the following season. The magistrate who received the anonymous letter handed it to the police and, having done so, discreetly pursued his own enquiries. The postmark, the nature of the notepaper used and the handwriting enabled him to trace the writer – Mme Vuagniaux, wife of a local artist.

In the course of further seances Mme Vuagniaux gave

more specific information. The doctor, she said again, had died in a rock cavity on a precipice close to a house that served as shelter for flocks of sheep when overtaken by the rain. Mme Vuagniaux and her husband were so convinced by the detail of their 'communications' that they decided to search for the body themselves, but a farmer, Antoine Lacquin, venturing to a part he rarely visited, found the doctor's body where he had fallen. The doctor's money and train ticket were near. He had fallen about fifty yards away from the base of a precipice.

The impressive feature of the long series of detailed communications given to the police is that they referred to details of a spot never visited by tourists and hardly ever by the farmer himself – for example, to a cavity in the precipice whose existence was until then unknown.

Although conveyed by means less usual than a dream or waking vision, Mme Vuagniaux had achieved a startling feat of true precognition. Nothing could account for the accuracy of the complicated picture of where the body of Dr Peterson would be – and was – found.

Although the man who had a vision of the Sunderland stranglings felt impelled to call upon the police and tell them of his experience, and although the police do receive various communications of this kind, more crimes are seen in precognitive visions or dreams than one might suppose. There is no true register of them; people usually keep such things to themselves, and where they do not, they often only tell a few people. My reason for saying that the proportion of dreams must be bigger than is generally supposed is the fairly large number of accounts in my possession which have never been published, or registered in any way. These have been sent to me only when I have, by one means or another, made known my deep interest in the subject.

Mrs Fay Brown, of Weeke, in Hampshire, was so disturbed by certain recurrent dreams in which murder featured that she wrote to the inspector in charge of the 'nude murders' case in the sixties, because there were certain coincidences she thought might be of help. Understandably, as the information was of too general a nature to provide a factual lead, she received little more than a letter of polite thanks, and an intimation that in such cases circumstantial evidence is not enough.

Even so, it is interesting to note that Mrs Brown had four or five dreams which began in 1964 and continued for a period of five months. In her dream, she was walking along the bank of a river. Although it was very dark, she could still see the water. She was with a man whom she could describe quite clearly – aged about thirty-five and slightly built, with fair hair, 'heavy features', dark trousers and a tweed sports coat. 'In my dream', she tells me, 'I said to the man "This is nice – where is it?" He answered, "This is the Thames at Hammersmith." We walked on a few yards and he said, "Go into the water and see if she is dead". I turned and walked into the river fully clothed. I walked in about six or seven yards and saw a young woman floating on her back. She had longish dark brown hair streaming out behind her and a light stocking tied around her neck. She was dead. I came out of the river and said to the man "Yes, it's OK She's dead all right". He turned and walked away to a white car and drove off.

'Three days later I heard of the first nude murder, of Hannah Tailford, whose body was pulled from the Thames at Hammersmith.'

There were other nude murders, mostly of prostitutes, many of whom were dark and slight. Later on, in further dreams, Mrs Brown dreamed of the man again. She was with him, high up on the roof of a church, from which he fell or jumped. Some years later, Mrs Brown read that suspects were narrowed down to about three men, one of whom (obviously not named, since he had living relatives) committed suicide.

These curious and unwelcome dreams were disturbing enough to induce Mrs Brown to inform the police about them, irrespective of whether they could be held to contain any nucleus of tangible information or not.

A young Nottingham student, Miss Jennifer Cridge, of Bramcote Hills, dreamed, on Thursday 18 December 1974, that she was in a huge London store in which there was a bomb scare and only a ten-minute warning. 'I told my mother,' she informs me, 'who laughed and said rubbish. On Sunday morning I picked up the *Sunday Express* to find that Harrods had had a bomb and ten minutes warning.'

Miss Cridge did not dream of Harrods specifically. It was a large store of the Harrods type. She had had previous and interestingly evidential dreams with a precognitive content – for example, 'a red car coming to pick me up outside my house.

We had a limey-green 1300 car. Days later,' she said, 'after telling my mother about the dream, Dad, who had previously said that he would not get a new car for ages, said he wanted a white 1800, but the dealer said that if he waited prices would go up, but that he could have a red car at the old price. He had no knowledge of this at all, but I knew it was going to happen ...'

The notorious kidnapping and murder of Mrs Muriel Makay, whose husband worked for the *News of the World*, was the subject of a dream experienced by Mr A. Whitten, a toolmaker living at Romeyn Road, South London. In his sleep he heard a voice saying: 'Look for two Indians with a blue van.' The sentence meant absolutely nothing to him, although, because of its unusual nature and what seemed to be the 'reality' of the voice, the memory stayed with him when he awoke. Later he heard the news of the Makay kidnapping. Several weeks later two Pakistanis were arrested for the murder. They had used a blue van for the abduction.

Incidentally, Mr Whitten had a dream in which he saw a headline (in September 1974) 'ALI WINS IN THE TENTH'. 'I wasn't thinking about him or the fight,' he wrote to me before the match took place. He was very nearly right: Mohammed Ali won in the *ninth* round.

# 11   Tricks of Time

On the evening of 4 September 1974, Mr A.H. Burchell of Market Drayton, Shropshire, a retired prison officer, was at home writing a letter to a friend when, for no reason that he can give, there 'suddenly came a flash' before his eyes which said: 'Tragedy at SAIGON'. The word 'Saigon' was in big capital letters.

'There was no indication', he told me, 'of date or time, nor any indication of the kind of tragedy, but the word SAIGON was so big and plain that I felt it must be something important. I promptly made a note of it on the back of my writing pad.' Vietnam had of course been in the news for many tragic years. But other countries had had their share of tragedy too. The emphasis was as puzzling to Mr Burchell as was the visual phenomenon itself. He listened to the news every day and followed the papers. Then, in the *Daily Express* of 16 September he saw a five-line report:

SAIGON:
All 71 people died when a Vietnamese
hijacker blew up a South Vietnam National
Airlines Boeing 707 with
two hand grenades.

Mr Burchell draws no arbitrary conclusions from this strange affair, and neither do I, but the coincidence as well as the unusual visual flash are certainly interesting. He adds: 'Although I have spent many years in the Far East, I have never been in Saigon, nor have I had any interest there.'

A lady in Gloucestershire, who gave permission (as all

informants have done whose identity is given) to be mentioned by name, but whose anonymity I nevertheless feel should be preserved, since she is happily married and has a family, relates a circumstance which she now believes was precognitive of a suicide:

> I was going with an RAF officer who idolized me. We quarrelled (my fault) and I told him to go away. I would not answer his letters or telephone calls. I meant to, eventually. I was just trying to be nasty. Anyway, the terrible thing was, he committed suicide.
>
> About ten days before this happened a ring I was wearing fell off my finger in two pieces – split straight through. A visitor in the house was horrified and said, 'You are going to lose someone close to you'. Also, about two weeks before, I had a pack of cards belonging to my former boyfriend, and all of a sudden I had an impulse to cut them. I did, and it was the Ace of Spades. This frightened me and I shuffled them and cut them again. It was the same card. The next night something told me to try again. I did not actually look at the cards, just towards them, and I cut the Ace again and again. My boyfriend and I had talked about Donald Campbell (the racing motorist) cutting the cards like this before he met *his* death.

That of course was not 'a glimpse of the future'. She did not visualize her fiancé taking his life. She merely had a premonition, based on an interpretation of alleged omens, that something unpleasant was certain to happen. She herself remains convinced that the two matters were related.

Miss Pauline Mewis, of Napier Street in Leicester, a catering assistant in the postgraduate medical centre, had a curious case of a precognitive flash which was witnessed by a companion while they were on night duty.

> After 2 a.m. I switched the radio over to police messages. It was sometime before Christmas when a description of a missing person came through. I said a name out loud and blow me if it wasn't the same name with the description. The night cook was with me listening in and I told her that I didn't know what made me say the name …

Mrs Cheryl Appleby of Chessington, Surrey, dreamed twenty-four hours before the event of unusually thorough – if not theatrical – security precautions at Heathrow airport. She saw the Israeli Ambassador very clearly and 'knew' (as one feels one knows in dreams) that there was a plot to put a bomb on the aircraft. 'I saw the man who was going to do this quite clearly: he was dressed in overalls like an airport worker. I didn't know about the airport check until I saw it all on television news the next day, and I was so worried that I wanted to tell the police, but felt that they might think me mad, so I didn't. Later I saw the Minister stepping out of the plane as I had seen him in my dream, but fortunately he was all right ...'

Rather similar to the 'flash' that made Mr Burchell expect something to happen in Saigon, so Mrs A.C. Warwood, a Dorking housewife, had an odd experience while sitting in a train at London's Charing Cross station when the word 'BOMB' moved slowly across the window. Four days later the first 'train bomb' occurred.

The same informant dreamed, on the night of Sunday 13 October 1974:

> ...that I was in a farmyard ... there were lots of cows and bulls being transported in a conveyor, like coal-mine trucks on wheels. Suddenly a big white bull appeared with large horns. He came slowly towards me and I was terrified, but kept very calm. I was thinking that any minute now he would charge. He came nearer and lowered his head and touched me slightly. He had wild red eyes which were looking at me full of hatred. I backed away but he came again and his horns poked into my left leg. The pain was awful. But I kept calm and the air was hushed and silent. He came again and this time he really dug his horns into me. I looked down and there were four round black bruises on my leg near the groin. I woke up quite expecting to feel the pain but, of course, I did not. The pain seemed intense and I felt that it was I who had been gored and not the bullfighter reported in yesterday's papers and today's. The *Sun*'s first reports were on Tuesday 15 October and again, with a picture, on Wednesday 16 October. I told my husband as soon as I awoke and confirmed in front of my mother what I had told him before they saw the cutting.

An intended suicide was prevented by a magistrate's 'hunch' some years ago. Mrs E.H. Rushford, at one time chairman of Durham magistrates, once had sent to jail – for a first offence – a young church organist who had forged his brother's name on a cheque to buy presents for a girl. On the morning of his release from prison, Mrs Rushford felt uneasy, and found it impossible to dismiss him from her mind. She felt impelled to go to the local railway station, where she saw him standing apart from other people. On speaking to him, she discovered with a shock how true her misgivings had been – he was there with the intention of throwing himself under a train. Her willingness to act on her 'hunch' certainly saved his life.

Unhappily, *two* of the Boston Strangler's victims who had respectively the strongest possible premonitions of impending death did not act on their premonitions. Sophie Clark, a nineteen-year-old Black medical student, was so convinced that she (of the hundreds of thousands of women in Boston) was a likely victim of the strangler that she pleaded with her parents to transfer her to another medical school outside Boston. She became the strangler's sixth victim. Patricia Bissette, a 23-year-old secretary, told her boss and his wife of a terrible dream she had had, and which she could not erase from her mind. *In her dream* she awoke to find a man in bed with her, who said 'I am the Boston Strangler'. A few days later (31 December 1962) she was found dead in bed with three nylon stockings and a white blouse tied tightly round her neck.

Robberies and burglaries are quite often foreseen by the victims, these 'previews' being far more than mere apprehensions. Mrs Vivienne Coombe, of Gillingham in Kent, had such an experience in the summer of 1973 which proved accurately prophetic. She was accompanying a group of mothers from Belfast, who had been given a week's holiday on the south coast of England, when they were invited to Alresford Priory one evening for supper with the Carmelite Friars, in a very old pilgrim's hall. The group were Catholics, although Mrs Coombe is not. The time was 8.45 p.m. and the party had finished their evening meal, which was followed by community singing. Mrs Coombe writes:

A local friend had driven over to join us for the evening, and I had an overwhelming urge to ask her to check up on my home as she had to pass it on the return journey to hers. Simultaneously I 'saw' a man at my dressing-table holding my jewellery case while another was in my kitchen by the larder, although I could not see what he was doing. I had a nasty feeling of evil. The man was 'spotlit' – hands, clothes, face, even with sunglasses in the breast pocket of his blue shirt! We had just had a tour of the grounds, and I knew no phone boxes were in sight. Neighbours here aren't on the phone and had I rung the police, crackpot apart, they would not have been in time. So I put it all out of my mind. That was Tuesday. My husband had been away and he returned on Friday evening to find the place ransacked.

Subsequent police enquiries proved how accurate her prevision had been. It was established that the burglary happened at about 8.45 on the Tuesday when the strong feeling had assailed her. One neighbour deposed to having seen a strange car in the Coombe house drive as she got home from choir duty at about that time. Another had seen the car as she passed by on her way home, and had reason to remember the time as the *Liver Birds* programme finished on television at 9 p.m. and she then packed her sons off to bed.

Here is a borderline precognition. Did Mrs Coombe see what was *just about to happen*, or see it while it was happening? If the latter, did Mrs Coombe 'pick up' by the process which for convenience is called telepathy, her friend's thoughts or misgivings – or was this a brief 'out-of-the-body' experience of the sort collected with such care by that eminent scientist and psychical researcher, Dr Robert Crookall of Bath? This is a typical example of a paranormal happening which cannot rigidly be classified without unwarranted dogmatism. Precognition – telepathy – out-of-the-body experience? It could be any, or all combined.

Mrs Coombe comments: 'Each and every time I get precognitive flashes, I also get a positive awareness that what I am receiving is absolutely correct – i.e. some details may be hazy or subject to misinterpretation but the essence is not of 'maybe' but 'positively'. From my own many instances I know ESP and precognition to be real and not wishful thinking.'

In 1968 the actress Moira Redmond received an advance warning of a burglary, although by way of dream and not, as in the foregoing story, by way of a visionary flash. So convinced was she that she asked an actor who lived above her in Talgarth Road, Hampstead, to keep an eye on her flat. He heard a window being forced open. He went down, knocked on her door (she was working at Bray studios at the time) and spoke to a man who was inside for a few minutes. Being suspicious, the actor, Robert Desmond, rang for the police and the man was arrested. Mr Desmond rang Moira Redmond at the studios to say, 'Your dream seems to be coming true!'

A particularly unpleasant example of precognition is the recorded and attested experience of Ian Stephens, who in 1956 awoke in his room at King's College, Cambridge, to see a realistic vision of a corpse hanging head downwards from one of the towers of the college chapel.

The hallucination, if such it was, so upset him, despite all his efforts to reassure himself after getting up at 8 a.m., that when he met the college's Second Bursar later in the day he mentioned his vision. The Second Bursar, Claude Sclater, thought it a most peculiar dream for anyone to have, but told Stephens that unpleasant dreams were not so very uncommon and he should not allow himself to be disturbed by it. He added that, by a coincidence, he was about to climb the scaffolding to inspect repair work. As most readers will know, King's College Chapel, with its soaring stone roof, is one of the most splendid examples of Perpendicular architecture in England. 'Night climbing' – risking life and limb in the stillness of the night by ascending the heights and soaring pinnacles – has been for generations a student tradition, however severely discouraged by the college authorities. That climbing should have woven itself into the dreams of a Cambridge student is not really so remarkable. However, Ian Stephens implored Sclater to take special care.

The student's vehemence did impress Sclater, who recorded the circumstances in his diary on 18 January 1956. Four days later, in the stillness of the early morning, when it was still dark, the Revd Ivor Ramsay, Dean of King's College, threw himself from the college roof.

Mrs Lorna Middleton, one of the numerous people who foresaw the Aberfan disaster, is one of those comparatively rare people for whom precognition is seemingly a regular occurrence. Mrs Middleton was one of the informants who contacted the late Dr J.C. Barker, a member of the Society for Psychical Research and a distinguished psychiatrist, when he was trying to establish, by encouraging correspondents and informants to contact him, whether the Aberfan disaster had, so to speak, cast its shadow before. He told me that he found Mrs Middleton one of his most convincing informants – and there were many who had in various ways foreseen the collapse of the slag-heap on Pantglass Junior School.

In general, Mrs Middleton's forecasts seem to be concerned with natural disasters and the more fearsome type of man-made accident, although they have included assassinations. Some of her predictions are in such general terms that they do not conform to what I regard as the reasonable constituents of true precognition. I am thinking in particular of her local newspaper, the *Tottenham and Edmonton Weekly Herald*, in which she wrote: (on 25 February 1970) 'I awoke this morning and I kept hearing the words "somebody is going to be shot". It appears to be connected with a famous person, dark skin.' The *Evening News* of London reported on 28 February 1970: 'Three shot in gun terror on earl's estate. Three people were blasted in their beds by a shotgun intruder at a cottage on an earl's estate today – shortly after fire swept through part of his ancestral home. The estate was Lord Fortescue's fruit farm.' Likewise the *Evening Standard* of 16 March 1970 reported that in Cyprus the former Minister of the Interior, Polycarpos Georgadjis, had been found shot in his car, on a country road about six miles outside Nicosia.

Mrs Middleton predicted on 27 September 1968 that a

tragic event would attend upon the Mexico Olympics. She conveyed her strong foreboding to her local newspaper, which carried the headline 'MEXICO TRAGEDY FORE-TOLD'. Days later came the news that fifteen people had died and hundreds had been injured in clashes between the police and troops and rioting students in Mexico City.

A sad and specific precognition of a shooting is recorded by Father Pedro Meseguer of Madrid. He received the information directly and of its authenticity there is no question. It also has that degree of *information not easily anticipated* which distinguishes precognition from fanciful fears, foreboding, superstitious apprehensions and vague, unformulated misgivings:

> Father N. was being sheltered in a house in Madrid during the Spanish Civil War. One day there was one of those fateful searches and the householder, a young married man, was taken away.
>
> They all felt he was going to be shot, but did not know it for certain. In fact, many people who were taken away escaped with their lives. In any case, they decided to call his father, who was living in a nearby town. He arrived, and as he came into the house he said, 'I know why you have called me. You needn't pretend: they have shot my son. I saw him shot in a dream, *with five others, and he was the only one who had a coffin.*' No one in the house knew anything of this, but they eventually found out that he had in fact *been shot with five others, and that he was the only one lying in a coffin,* thanks to an uncle of his who had heard of his execution and had a coffin made for him.

Over a century ago a precognitive dream of unusual detail presaged, but did not prevent, a murder. However, it did encompass the arrest and execution of the killers, at a time when justice was swift and condign, when the West really was wild and woolly.

The owner of the Luna Hotel in Lewiston, Idaho, had a terrible nightmare concerning a friend, a miner called Lloyd Magruder, who often stayed at his hotel. He saw, as in a play enacted, his friend savagely attacked by three companions, had a close-up of the killer's face as he wielded the axe, so savagely that he could not extricate its blade from the victim's body except by putting his foot upon his chest and pulling with all his might.

Lloyd Magruder was set upon by his three companions, James Romaine, D.C. Lowry and David Howard, while camping one night at Clearwater. Their object was the theft of his fortune – a considerable fortune then – thirty-five thousand golden dollars and a freight wagon laden with valuables. With equal ferocity they killed four others and, wrapping them in their own sleeping blankets, flung their bodies into a deep canyon nearby.

The sad thing is that, after his dream and *prior to this tragedy*, Bill Leachy had seen the murderer in the flesh. For the following day the Walla Walla stage coach arrived, and among those who came into the Luna Hotel to buy tickets for the journey was Lowry, whose face was identical with the man seen in the dream as wielding the axe. But just as today you could hardly detain somebody because they had figured in a dream you happened to have had, so Bill Leachy had to keep his distressing information to himself. He knew he would have been laughed to scorn if he had tried to enlist the interest of the law at that stage.

Later, hearing that pack-horses had been left to their own devices at Clearwater and were running wild, Leachy persuaded the sheriff to go with him to the ranch to investigate. There they found evidence of crime, for Magruder's saddle was lying on the ground, in the canyon.

The culprits were arrested in San Francisco, tried in Idaho and hanged on 4 March 1865.

Perhaps the feature, gruesome as it is, that distinguishes this story is the part of Leachy's dream in which the murderer put his foot to his victim's chest for leverage by which to retrieve his embedded axe. When Magruder's body was found, Lowry's bloody footprint was clearly impressed upon his chest.

Back in England, an extraordinary story unfolded at an inquest held in Norwich during October 1972, on the body of a woman found on a Norfolk beach. Mr John Birch of Beach Road, Scratby, awoke at home to see on the ceiling the face of a woman; when he looked harder, it vanished, but not before he had familiarized himself with its essential details. The experience was, naturally, a shock and a surprise to him, but it was to have special significance for him when he found the body of the woman when walking near the waterline *three days later*. The body, which had been washed ashore, looked as if it could be that of a middle-aged French woman, but on one point there was no doubt in his mind. *The face was the face he had seen on his ceiling.*

A case of murderers being detected by clairvoyance is on record at the Central Premonitions Bureau in New York. Mrs Mildred Barton, a Cincinnati housewife, forecast that three men and a woman were involved in a notorious murder, and at the time she sent in her forecast the FBI had no clues to go upon. Three weeks later three men were arrested, and a fortnight afterwards a woman was also indicted. The clairvoyant, who had absolutely no direct or indirect knowledge of the affair, was proved right.

People who are to be murdered have – in a minority of cases, it would seem – precognitions of their impending end. Two weeks before William Jones, a tall, bearded labourer, of Cantwell Road, London, was murdered he awoke screaming from a terrible nightmare in which he had seen a man coming towards him with a knife, and thrusting it into his chest. His mother, Pat Jones, told him that the dream might be intended as a warning, and urged him to be careful and keep clear of trouble. To this, he merely laughed and told her not to be stupid. The killing, incidentally, occurred only a hundred yards from his home.

In 1967, ex-Scotland Yard detective James Axon, in a new role as Chief of Police on the Island of Jersey, was surprised to receive a flying visit from Mrs Lillian Hook of Finland, whose daughter had been found brutally murdered on the island. The surprise lay not so much in the fact of her coming to see what had happened – that was normal enough – but in her report that on the night her daughter was murdered she had seen her in a dream, looking very distressed, and had also seen her murderer, whom she described as being short, about thirty, with dark hair and a sloping forehead. Tuula Hook, who was twenty, was found battered to death after being last seen talking to a car-driver. A curious feature of this case is that her mother, on visiting police headquarters in Jersey, was entirely familiar, as by a kind of *déjá vu*, with the room and the layout there.

An American psychic, Dr Alexander Tanous – born in Lebanon forty-nine years ago – has helped the USA police with clues which he has picked up clairvoyantly. For example, when an eight-year-old boy, John Nason, disappeared from his home in Freeport, Maine, and was later found suffocated, Tanous sketched a murder suspect for the police with no knowledge of his identity. Tanous had been consulted at the request of the boy's parents and relatives. The Maine Department Police Chief, Herman Boudreau, was concentrating on four key suspects at the time and wished to see if the psychic's sketch would 'match' any of the four people he had in mind. After giving several clues, Tanous produced a sketch of the man he felt was the culprit – it tallied with the description, which the police possessed but did not reveal, of Milton I. Wallace.

Police Chierf Boudreau took a chance – he decided to accuse a suspect of the crime. With the object of questioning the suspect, he raced off to his apartment, and there found the boy's decomposing body, under the bed, wrapped in a blanket, just as Tanous had told them. 'What he had told us,' Police Chief Boudreau declared, 'put us on the right track.'

Tanous has been consulted by the police on over twenty cases, in eighteen of which his information has been of help in solving the crimes.

In his particular case, there is a general background of psychic predisposition, as both his parents were unusually intuitive. He is a teacher of theology, and does valuable work with the American Society for Psychical Research. He was tested by them for ESP capacities and found to score very high – there was only one chance in three thousand that his answers could be due to laws of chance.

Professor John Beloff, a former President of the Society

for Psychical Research and lecturer in psychology at the University of Edinburgh, has in his files the account of how Mrs Gwen Bridgland, of Abbey Road, London, dreamed *before it happened* of a murderer throwing himself under a train. Mrs Bridgland knew of this fourteen days before it occurred, and in her dream 'knew' the man was wanted for a sex murder.

# 12  Shadows of Disaster

One evening in late August 1975, I was working in my study at home when the telephone rang. It was a Mrs Lorna Middleton, one of many people who had experienced a precognition of the 1966 Aberfan disaster.

It was my friend the late Dr J.C. Barker, psychiatrist at Shelton Hospital, Shrewsbury, and the first doctor to reach Aberfan when the news of that disaster broke, who initiated a research project at that time. As he was interested in psychical research he wondered whether this event had cast its shadow before. He established that in twenty-four cases, not only had his informants had a precognition of the disaster, but they had corroboration of their claim to have done so. One of the most remarkable accounts was that of Mrs Middleton. Meeting Mrs Middleton with Dr Barker at that time, I arranged that she would keep me abreast of any strong precognitive hunches she might have from time to time. Hence her telephone call to me now.

'I have a strong feeling that a bomb is going off in Kensington, and perhaps Birmingham', she said. I noted it in my diary.

Three hours later I was playing cards when the ground and air shook with a sickening thud. One had heard that sound often enough during the war to know what it was. It was almost round the corner from my home. A bomb had exploded in the doorway of a shoe shop in Kensington Church Street. Captain Roger Goad, a forty-year-old bomb disposal officer awarded the MBE for his gallantry in Cyprus, lay dead in the road. The bomb had exploded while he was attempting to defuse it.

Mrs Middleton has, since Aberfan, recorded a great many predictions which have subsequently been fulfilled. She forecast a tornado which struck the west coast of the United States in 1967, and predicted that tragedy would attend upon the Soviet spaceship in which Komerov died.

Of course Mrs Middleton did not specifically state that the bomb I heard explode would go off in any particular street, nor specify the time. Even so, some of her precognitive visions are sometimes quite detailed. Thus, she telephoned me at 3.45 p.m. on 16 July 1975, to say that she could see 'a man in a tunnel surrounded by water'. Naturally, the message conveyed nothing to me; it later emerged that frogmen hunting for clues to the Black Panther, murderer of the kidnapped Lesley Whittle, had probed the thick mud in a three-hundred-yard stretch of tunnel and found several small items relevant to the killing. The search was possible because the water level in that tunnel had dropped.

Earlier in the year Mrs Middleton had written to me: 'I keep hearing the name Princess Margaret over and over again'. Some months later, while on a visit to Australia, Princess Margaret was distressed to hear that Brian Finemore, the art expert who was to have been her guide on an art gallery tour, had been found murdered in his flat a mile from the National Gallery in Victoria, hardly more than an hour before Princess Margaret's visit.

On 7 October 1975 Mrs Middleton reported to me that she had awakened with a 'terrible choking feeling' comparable with that which she had experienced at the time of Aberfan. Two days later the London *Evening News* reported that a school bus carrying seventy children had crashed down a hillside at Pietersburg, South Africa, killing thirty-four of them. Both tragedies involved a large number of children, and both involved a hillside.

Mr Stuart Andrews, a London advertising executive, whom I have mentioned before in another context, dreamed on 14 May 1971, of a dance floor collapsing. He related his dream, which had been a vivid one, to two people, one of them an executive in a printing firm and the other a friend. Two days later, a dance-hall floor collapsed in France. There were striking coincidences between the dream and the occurrence, although oddly enough, Mr Andrew's dream was associated with Tooting, London and not with France.

Mrs Barbara Winspear of Elton Road, Billingham, Cleveland, is a secretary. Her hobbies are reading, singing and further education, and she is not a member of any organization interested in the occult or psychical research.

On 1 June 1974, a disaster occurred at Flixborough, on Humberside Down, at the Nypro Chemical plant. By an unhappy 'chain of errors', as the official report had it, twenty-eight people were killed. The explosion that killed them was caused by a temporary pipe failing. The pipe had been installed as a rush job after one had been removed because of a leak. There was, the Committee of Enquiry found, 'no proper design study, no proper consideration of the need for support, no safety testing, no reference to the relevant British Standard'. And there was no proper works engineer, although a service engineer acted as co-ordinator. As a result of the pipe failure, large quantities of cyclohexane, used in the manufacture of plastic, were released, mixing with the air to form a deadly explosive vapour cloud. The blast was equivalent to forty-five tons of TNT. Mrs Winspear told me:

> I awoke around 5 a.m. on that particular morning, and had had a terrible dream. I dreamed I was in the laboratory of a chemical works, and a man in a white overall (unbuttoned) was standing over a container or hole and looking into it. The next second there was a flash of blue and *a huge cloud of vapour or mist* – it was white – engulfed the room. People ran for their lives, including me, and I was frightened. I escaped, but remember looking back on the scene and 'seeing' a black figure with arms outstretched, clutching at a grille over a door or window. I remember distinctly the blue, the white, the black and the red. It was horrific. I told my husband this at lunch-time. At tea-time the Flixborough disaster happened.

John Buckmaster, of Scholars Road, Chingford, Essex, is a legal executive in his early thirties. He has no special predisposition to the uncanny or occult, belongs to no organization of an occult, mystical or 'way out' character, and pursues such harmless hobbies as reading and amateur dramatics.

In the summer of 1967, he had what he describes as a 'short waking dream' in colour:

> I saw a large building in extensive grounds. The building was on fire and there were people running. This occurred when I was in bed at night, just before I was going to sleep.
>
> On the following day I heard on the television news that a nearby mental hospital had had a fire in which one patient died.

The hospital was Claybury Hospital, Woodford Bridge, Woodford Green, Essex and the curious thing was that for some months Mr Buckmaster had been attending Group Therapy in the Day Clinic at the hospital – not for any mental disability but merely to get 'over the hump' of a minor nervous depletion occasioned, as happens to so many thousands of people, by overwork.

Mr Buckmaster was at this time a solicitor's managing clerk in a local firm, and was extremely surprised to be informed by his secretary that the patient who had died in that hospital fire had been identified as an ex-client of his. He had acted for him about a year earlier in a claim for compensation arising from an accident: 'Almost as soon as my secretary told me this, I said that his parents would soon be in to see me, and not long after they did call. This, perhaps, was only to be expected but, somehow, I *knew* they would call …'

I agree with him that his expectation that his ex-client's parents would come and see him following the tragedy of their son's death was not especially remarkable. But the coincidence – if coincidence it were – of the dream and the happening is certainly interesting.

Mrs Irene Jones, sub-postmistress at Carnmenellis, near Redruth in Cornwall, is in her fifties and was for many years a Red Cross VAD. Although she had this particular experience thirty years ago, the memory of it remains with her still. She was living in Porchester, near Portsmouth, at the time. She had a dream that the Bristol Hippodrome was on fire, and that all of one side came crashing down. The dream was in colour, and bright, and the sense of heat and menace very real. As her sister was living in Bristol at the time, Mrs Jones wrote to her, only to be told as is fairly usual in such cases, that she had 'imagined it'. But within several weeks, the fire which had made so vivid an impression upon her actually happened.

Carl Gustav Jung (1875-1961), the Swiss psychiatrist who helped to found analytical psychology, was decidedly more religious and mystical than his equally distinguished friend, Sigmund Freud. Jung's conception of a universal consciousness, a kind of pool that retains all that was and all that is, allows some basis for precognition, a phenomenon which he himself experienced at times, and on other occasions even practised. Consider, for example, his prevision of the First World War:

> Toward the autumn of 1913 the pressure which I had felt was in me seemed to be moving outward, as though it were something in the air. The atmosphere actually seemed to be darker than it had been. It was as though the sense of oppression no longer sprang exclusively from a psychic situation, but from concrete reality.
>
> In October, while I was away on a journey, I was suddenly seized by an overpowering vision: I saw a monstrous vision covering all the northern and low-lying lands between the North Sea and the Alps. When it came up to Switzerland I saw that the mountains grew higher and higher to protect our country. I realized that a frightful catastrophe was in progress. I saw the mighty yellow waves, the floating rubble of a civilization and the drowning bodies of countless thousands. Then the whole sea turned to blood. The vision lasted about one hour. I was perplexed and nauseated and ashamed of my weakness.

Two weeks afterwards the vision recurred, under similar conditions and even more vividly than before, the blood more emphasized than ever. An inner voice spoke: '*Look at it well; it is wholly real, and it will be so.*'

Jung had numerous precognitive experiences of a personal nature. Once he dreamed that his wife's bed was a deep pit with stone walls – in other words, a grave. He heard a deep sigh, as of one dying. The shade or phantasm of his wife floated upwards from the pit, and he noted she was wearing a white gown interwoven with curious black symbols. Jung awoke, roused his wife, and checked the time.

'The dream', he recalled, 'was so curious that I thought it might signify a death.'

It did. He had noted the time of the dream – 3 a.m. At seven o'clock he received news that a cousin of his wife had died at three o'clock that morning.

Sometimes, as Jung observed, precognition could manifest itself with some identifying factor missing. This could be disturbing, as in a dream in which his sister, who had died some years previously, and a friend who had died, appeared. They were with a lady who, in his dream he associated with Basle. But try as he might he could not recall who she was. He tried thinking of all the people he knew in Basle, but not one measured up to his recollection of her appearance. A few weeks later a friend of his – the one name and person, of all he knew in Basle, whom he had been unable to recall – was killed in a fatal accident.

From these and other experiences, and from the deep conviction that there is a spiritual core and kernel to all life and living, Jung concluded: 'There are indications that at least part of the psyche is not subject to the laws of space and time.'

Vic Jones, who lives in Margaret Close, Brightlingsea, Sussex, is a nightshift worker for a firm that prints *Psychic News*. Printing is just his job. He doesn't by inference endorse, or become influenced, by the material that goes into type, any more than he would need to be a sheep to be a judge of mutton. Even so, he found himself unwittingly, getting a preview of a terrible train tragedy which was to shock Londoners just before Christmas 1974.

His first unpleasant dream of a train crash was on 2 December. It was so vivid that, instead of being speedily erased from his memory as dreams generally are, it left an unpleasant 'hangover' which cast a gloom. He tried to forget it, but the next night the same dream recurred. He

saw a busy railway station, with hundreds of people laden
with Christmas presents hurrying about to catch their
trains. He looked up (in his dream) at the station's name
board and read distinctively 'PADDINGTON'.

Next, in a moment of horror, he was surveying the scene
of the crash. There was a train wrecked, people, presents
and shopping were strewn about everywhere. And connected with the scene were the figures 16/23, which upon
waking, he assumed might provide a clue as to when the
accident would occur. Worried about this strange and
unwelcome information, he confided in a fellow worker,
Robert Ward. Sensibly, Ward suggested that he should
write down the details of his dreams. This Mr Jones did,
and the account was then placed in a sealed envelope, and
the envelope, signed and dated, was put in a locker.

Obviously neither *hoped* this awful dream would come
true. The point of these advance precautions was to be sure
that Mr Jones would not need to rely upon his memory, nor
convince anybody that the information contained in his
dream was in his possession at a particular time. On the
morning of 20 December, Mr Jones opened his morning
paper and saw that his dream had, alas, been precognitive.
A train packed with commuters and Christmas shoppers
had jumped the rails while running twelve minutes late just
past Ealing Broadway in west London, on its journey from
*Paddington* to Reading and Oxford. The diesel motor had hit
a snag on the side of the track and fallen on its side. Ten
people were killed and fifty injured.

An unusual example of *retrocognition* was related to me
by Shaun Hennessy, a photo-journalist, from Bingham
Crescent, Barnstable, Devonshire:

> I remembered the day when as a child, I came out of my
> first-floor bedroom one morning to see a piece of rope tied
> around a bannister rail. I asked my mother why she had
> 'put it there.' She looked alarmed. On going back with her
> – nothing was to be seen!
>
> But she did tell me a fact that I had never been told
> before – that the previous occupant of the house had hung
> herself from the same rail ten years before! At that time I
> dismissed my 'vision' as imagination.

The story of the *Titanic* has been frequently related. The White Star liner, described as the safest vessel afloat, struck an iceberg off Cape Race, Newfoundland, on the night of 14/15 April 1912 and sank with a loss of 1,517 lives.

Many people had a prevision of that disaster. Mrs Marshall, wife of the well-known sportsman, Jack Marshall, went hysterical with anxiety as the ship steamed through the English Channel. Shaw Desmond, in *My Adventures in the Occult* describes, as one of his three 'Adventures in Time', the day he walked with W.T. Stead, editor of the *Review of Reviews*, shortly before Stead was to join the *Titanic* for her maiden voyage. Shaw Desmond had so overpowering a premonition of the vessel's disaster and Stead's death that he wrote it in his diary. Stead was, in fact, one of those who died. When somebody told Desmond that Vanderbilt, the American millionaire, had been saved, and that possibly W.T. Stead had also been saved, he was emphatic that this was not so. He had a distinct vision of his friend awash in icy waters, and told his wife flatly: 'he is not saved. He is drowned.'

I will not pursue at further length this classic of sea disasters, but the following account, never before published, from a surviving passenger of the *Titanic*, James H. Lawler, of Ruskin, Florida, is interesting even today:

I was born in 1897. From March 1909 to September 1913 I was resident at the Training Ship Mercury, in Hamble, Hampshire, England, under the educator and athlete Charles Burgess Fry (C.B. Fry, the famous cricketer). One Saturday I had to go to the dentist in Southampton to have a wisdom tooth removed. The dentist had to give me gas, but for some reason or other had to have another man with him to administer the gas. He waited an hour or more for this chap to show up.

This is the picture of that hour's wait. The dentist's office was on the second or third floor of the building, in the back with a window facing the Solent. Out in the fairway was moored the *Titanic* directly in front of our view. Small boats were running back and forth, carrying people wishing to view the ship. I would have been more interested in battleships, because that was what I was in training for.

Whatever conversation took place was about the Biggest and Unsinkable ship.

Finally I was under the anaesthetic, still looking at the *Titanic*. The number of boats increased by the dozen. People were going on board in their hundreds. They didn't seem to go below, but stayed on the promenade decks until they were full to overflowing. So many people were jammed on board that many more were hanging over the rails. When the ship could hold no more she started to list to port, towards us. She continued to list until she had capsized and all the people were in the water.

I have no recollection of going under or coming out of the anaesthetic but the moment the ship had turned turtle I was out of the chair and running to the window and being restrained by the dentist. He thought something had gone wrong with me. I was shaken so badly that even the sight of the *Titanic*, sitting as majestically as she was before, failed to calm me.

Four days later we of the *Mercury* got up early and marched down the Hamble to the Solent shore. There we 'fell in' and cheered as she passed. Four days later she sank.

Mr Lawler's experience raises the interesting question of whether extra-sensory perception (ESP) is activated, or heightened, by anaesthetics or drugs.

Mrs Catherine Wilmott, of Eye, Suffolk, recalls very vividly her precognition of the sinking by a German submarine of the *Lusitania* on 7 May 1915, when 124 American passengers lost their lives. She was only a small child at the time. She told me:

I have seen many strange things happening in my dreams, which have come true later.

My first memory of these pre-happenings was when I was about four. I dreamt about a big ship sinking. There were lots of people shouting. I got up and put my coat and shoes on, and as I was going out of the door my mother woke up and quickly caught hold of me. I told her I was going down to the beach because there was a big ship sinking and all the men couldn't get off. I wanted to tell the coastguard. Of course, my mother put me back to bed.

Three days later all Kingstown, an area of Dublin, heard that the *Lusitania* had sunk outside the harbour.

With the phenomenon of precognition one finds, again and again, that it is disasters and human calamities which send their echoes back, as it were, from the future – as though these happenings were predestined, allotted their specific place in the future, and somehow seen or anticipated by somebody in the present.

Mrs Petronella Palliser of Truro, Cornwall, tells me:

About eight years ago I dreamed about a car accident. I remember this especially as I had never dreamed of a car accident before. In these dreams (at least three) the accident was not at all serious. I felt like a spectator. A woman got out of a caravan and gave me and some other people a cup of tea. A fat constable driving a rather big, black motorcycle figured largely. Every time I slept again, he was there with his large, red face, wearing a black crash helmet with POLICE written on it.

The next day I was driving home, after delivering my sons, aged 12, 13 and 15, to some dunes with a picnic lunch (I used the car every day in the summer holidays). Anyway, I was driving not more than 30 m.p.h. down a narrow twisting country lane when a large Jaguar came round a bend on the wrong side of the road and smashed into my car. I was thrown out, but only bruised.

*Presently a large fat policeman on a black bike wearing a black crash helmet arrived. A woman got out of a caravan and offered tea to me and the other driver.*

On the night of 29 October 1972, Mrs Robert Page of Crooks, Sheffield, was in bed with her husband when she was disturbed by an unusually vivid dream. She was driving along a lonely road and coming to the scene of a car crash, where several people were hurt. She got out of her car and hurried to the scene to assist (she is a State Registered Nurse at the Children's Hospital in Sheffield) and as she gave first aid, she could see another car approaching the scene. This other car stopped and a young man emerged from it, to say 'My name's Ian.'

Being upset by the dream and its unpleasant realism,

she awakened her husband and told him of it, adding, 'I can't understand the reference to Ian. I don't know anybody of that name.'

Two days later, on Tuesday 31 October, Mrs Page, her husband Robert, Piers Barnes and his wife Jane, were driving on the moors between Sheffield and Fox House (on the outskirts of the village of Hathersage) when they came to the scene of an accident which had clearly occurred only a few minutes before they arrived. There had been a crash between two cars and two girls were injured. Mrs Page could see one staggering out of the car, streaming with blood and, thinking to herself, 'this is my dream, but this time it's real', she hurried forward and quickly rendered first aid. The essentials done, she remarked to her husband how extraordinary it was that all this had been foreseen two days ago, 'but,' she added, 'the bit about Ian doesn't come into it.' At the moment another car approached, a young man emerged from it and came hurrying forward. *'My name's Ian', he told them. 'Can I help?'*

Mrs May Merton of Holywell, Clwyd, Wales told me of an experience she had in 1945, when she was serving with the Women's Auxiliary Air Force in Shropshire. She was at that time engaged to an Australian flying officer whose forename was Alan, and who was an instructor at her station. They were happy in each other's company and looking forward to the war ending. At the end of April, he went over to the satellite station to ferry planes to other parts of the country as the war was in its closing stages.

We had to meet in Shrewsbury whenever possible, usually having a meal and seeing a film. On May 4th we met and went to see a film and went upstairs to the café in the cinema afterwards. As we sat opposite each other I felt the same feeling of admiration and adoration that I had felt long ago for my brother Colin. I tried to dismiss the feeling but it persisted. This time I knew it for what it was – a premonition that I would never see him again. Crossing the field from the village hall to the WAAF quarters I felt sure that he was in danger, but I was helpless to do anything about it.

I went on duty the following day and though the

weather was very bad with rain and heavy cloud, at approximately 11 a.m. I heard the Controller calling Alan's radio number, Two-Zero-Six. There was no reply. My friend Molly and I were on the homing unit and kept listening watch. I didn't make any enquiries, but when we came off duty the following day I was told that Alan was missing.

He was eventually found, having crashed in the Welsh mountains.

Mrs Merton's tragic premonition concerning her fiancé had a bizarre sequel. A tailor in Shrewsbury, whom they had visited together, was making him a suit. She called in on the tailor to tell him what had happened. The tailor had dreamt of the crash beforehand and ceased work on the suit, knowing that it would not be needed.

Mrs Gladys Baker of Woodgrange Drive, Southend-on-Sea, Essex, owes her life to ESP. In the spring of 1938 she had a dream in which there was a great deal of broken glass, and 'blood running in the gutter.'

She awoke shaken and depressed and her late husband, to cheer her up, gave her five shillings (a good deal of money then – worth about 150p in present purchasing terms) to buy some seeds at Woolworth's, since she was very fond of gardening. She decided to buy them at the High Street branch and the expedition was an exciting one, for in those days Woolworth's proud boast was 'Nothing in this store over sixpence' – and a huge range of goods were indeed on offer. Try and imagine today a large store with counter upon counter of goods with nothing costing more than two-and-a-half new pence!

Clutching her five shillings, Mrs Baker looked enviously into the window and its display of seed packets. But there was no hurry to buy, she suddenly thought. The whole purpose of her expedition was to buy seeds, yet now they were in front of her she felt, by some sudden instinct, she should go away.

I crossed the road. Opposite I heard the most awful crash, the sound of breaking glass and women screaming. A car had come up Alexander Street, turned into the High Street, and the driver accelerated three times and went through three Woolworth windows. I had just moved from the centre window. I looked round and there was my dream, broken glass everywhere and blood in the gutter. I should have probably been killed if I had not moved at that moment.

Mrs Sue Cole of Derby Road, Gloucester, had not only experienced several precognitive scenes, but lost her husband after he had had a precognition of his own death. Her first dream was so absurd in its content that its fulfilment makes it especially interesting.

> I dreamed I was sitting on a settee on a darkened stage with a young man I had known for a long time. We appeared to be listening to music and a variety show. About six months later I was approached to join a dramatic society. There I met the young man again (I had not seen him during this period). We did a play in which we sat on a settee in a darkened room and listened to a variety show exactly as I had dreamed – even to the position of the furniture.

During the war, Mrs Cole was attached to a barrage balloon site in Dagenham, Essex, during the 'doodle-bug' period of pilotless flying bombs. Having dreamed that the site had been hit by one, she detailed the girls to go into the shelters which, with a lot of grumbling, they did. Before long this site – No. 26 Cranbrook Road, Playing Fields, Ilford, Essex – was nothing but a hole in the ground.

People sometimes wonder whether, in the face of a strong premonition or precognitive dream, they should take some avoiding action. There is no simple answer to that, but I know of one instance where the teller of the story wished he had ignored the warning implied.

Thomas Carter, an inventor and designer, of Melling, near Liverpool, told me this story against himself:

> One day I saw a friend of mine walking across a car park to his car. Now on the previous night I had had an unpleasant dream about him being involved in an

accident. I at first hesitated to tell him, but then I thought I
had better. 'John!' I shouted. He turned around and started
to approach me, then he was suddenly knocked down by a
reversing car, but fortunately he was not hurt, just
shocked. He couldn't understand why I could not stop
laughing. You see, in my opinion, if I had not tried to warn
him about a possible accident, he would probably not have
had one.

Precognition may be short-term or long-term. Some vivid
impressions are received years before the event, but some
are imminent, as though some urgent instinct is secretly at
work, seeking to warn us. This was the experience, still
vividly remembered, of 67-year-old Ernest Oldham, of
Hollins, Middleton, Manchester.

> We were out on a Saturday night ride, five of us. We went
> into a pub, and after about two drinks I had this dull feeling
> come over me. It became worse, so being on my own, I
> asked Mrs Smethurst to come outside with me. When we
> got outside I had a picture of us all in the car going home,
> and in front of us were a crowd of youths, and I shouted
> 'Stop that car!' Then I went blank. I explained all this to
> Phyllis [Smethurst] but she laughed ... Two hours later it all
> happened and we almost killed four or five youths.

Mr H.J. Cleaver, of Colchester Road, Holland-on-Sea,
Essex, is a retired watchmaker. His work used to entail
much travel by train. From Belvedere in Kent to Clapham
Junction involved travelling in six trains for the return
journey, (Belvedere–London Bridge; London Bridge–
Waterloo; Waterloo to Clapham Junction). The point of
this detail is that he was clearly used to trains and had no
fear of them. He was in good health, and had no
disposition to nervousness or nervous disease, but:

> On my day off from work, which was a Wednesday, I
> would go to see my friend, a Mr B. Porter, who had a
> jeweller's shop in Hartley Wintney, Hampshire. On this
> particular Wednesday I had made a date to see him. *I got
> out of bed to dress and had a vivid mental picture of a train crash.
> I could see the train on its side and the back part of our train
> smashed up.* I must say this was so strong that I said to my

wife, who was still in bed, 'Shall I go today?' (Not telling her why I did not want to go.) She said, 'Well, why not? You have made the date to go!' I thought to myself: 'Why have I got so frightened?' So I went, and on the return journey to Waterloo from Basingstoke our train stopped just outside Fleet station and a train from Bournemouth ran into it. My carriage was smashed up. I was thrown out on to the line but was not badly hurt, I am glad to say, just a few pieces of glass through my ear, otherwise I was OK.

The train which hit us was *lying on its side* just as I saw it.

Michael Bentine, the famous television comedian, had not merely a premonition, but a clear precognition of his son's death in a plane crash. During the day he had a distinct 'vision' of an aircraft flying into a cloud and crashing to the ground.

So detailed and definite was this precognition that he told his son Stuart about it, in the presence of his mother, warning him to take care. Never before had Michael Bentine warned his son about anything, realizing as all sensible parents do that children must make their own judgements and learn to be confident about what they are doing – that they should not be moulded into dependence upon their parents, despite loving and close relationships. He knew individuals must make a free choice.

Stuart Bentine, an amateur pilot, died when the plane he was flying crashed at Petersfield, Surrey, on 28 August 1971.

I am indebted to the late Lord Ogmore (Lt-Col. David Rees Rees-Williams, PC, TD, JP) for an interesting story of how he foresaw the death of a brother officer in World War Two. Lord Ogmore was on active service from August 1939 to October 1945 and, incidentally, presided over the first General Military Court held in Britain. In 1943 he was sitting in the officer's mess of the Welsh anti-aircraft unit which he commanded when somehow the topic came up about whether the future could be foretold. A lieutenant in the Royal Artillery who had recently been transferred to the Commandos and was awaiting posting, asked Lord Ogmore if he would read his hand.

Lord Ogmore was disinclined to do so, but consented under pressure. The lieutenant's request, in any case, seemed odd and out of character – he was not the sort of man who would normally concern himself about such matters. He was a powerfully built man, a keen rugby football forward, and a businessman in civilian life. He was also in his middle thirties, rather old, Lord Ogmore thought to himself, for his rank in the Commandos.

'He was a married man,' Lord Ogmore says, 'but had fallen in love with an attractive ATS officer. He was cheerful, normally of equable temperament, and one of the best types of Englishmen. I liked him very much.'

> I took his hand and I knew, as it were instinctively, that before long he would be dead. I said nothing, however, and quietly he said to me, 'You see my death soon, don't you?' I replied that it was all nonsense and that I did not believe in palm-reading and that sort of thing, but he pressed me and reluctantly I admitted that I did feel he was going to be killed soon. He said quietly that he had had the same thing told him elsewhere. Shortly afterwards he was killed in a raid.

Mrs M. Bradfield, of Dereham, Norfolk, tells me that for years she has experienced powerful precognitions which come by way of *physical* sensation – 'a surge through my body, somehow through my feet up to my head, it's like a flash and does not last many seconds':

> One very close instance that happened a few years ago and is forever with me concerned my son Peter. He was returning to University after an Easter vacation. As I watched him drive away and before I turned into the house I knew I would never see him again. He was a fine, strong lad of twenty-one years and intending to become a doctor. He did very well in his exams, was a happy boy with no worries, loved good music and also *held certificates for swimming and flying solo* [my italics – author].
>
> On Friday, 4 June 1960 I just had to speak to Peter although he always wrote and phoned us once a week. He said 'Don't worry about me, Mum. I can take care of myself and will be coming home on 10 June'. But I was the last

person to speak to him or his friends who lost their lives with him. On Monday, 7 June, Peter went to bring back a yawl with his friends, as he was not taking an exam until the Wednesday and had time to spare. The yawl was found intact at 5.a.m. completely dry but the students were missing and remained so for fourteen days.

We were invited to visit some of his friends and they asked us to stay for dinner; I accepted. But again I had this surge shoot through me and knew I must return home at once. We had not been back in the house for many minutes before the police phoned to say that Peter's body had been picked up. Within days the other bodies were recovered. I was right. We did not see Peter alive again.

Peter Bradfield was an only son, but there is nothing to support the view that Mrs Bradfield was in any way over-anxious or over-possessive about him. There were no apparent reasons why she should have had misgivings about his safety.

A curious feature of this tragedy was that Peter and his companions set out to sail from Broughty Ferry to St Andrews, only eighteen miles, or six hours, away. The skipper of the dredger who found the *Strega* found she was upright, dry and everything on board, including the personal possessions of the crew, was neatly stowed. But its mast had broken off – it was picked up off the Angus coast. And although they left in good weather, they ran into thunderstorms and squalls.

# 13　What Lies Behind It All?

Since precognition is one of the most elusive of all psychic phenomena, it would be totally unreasonable for anyone to ask: what lies behind it all?

Unreasonable or not, it is a natural question to ask, even though it is a gross over-simplification. When we try to understand foreknowledge, we are faced, inevitably, with the complexities of time and its nature, of space-time and the quantum theory, and of the extent and limitations of human perception.

*All* of those phenomena classified, for convenience, as 'psychic' have eluded all scientific efforts to reduce them to an identifiable formula lending itself to repeatable experiment. Possibly we are near some sort of break-through as regards telepathy and, in fact, there are those who claim that it is no longer a mystery, but that the discovery of its secrets has been hushed up for defence purposes – since the implanting of information in the minds of others, and the surreptitious monitoring of the thoughts of people could have offensive and defensive uses. Telepathy properly understood and applied would be a formidable military weapon.

Other psychic phenomena, despite the millions of words written about them and the activities of scientists busying themselves in laboratories and educational institutions throughout the world are scarcely better understood than they were nearly a century ago, when the Society for Psychical Research was first founded.

My own researches have convinced me of two things: that precognition does occur and is a phenomenon to be taken seriously; and that the explanation for it, when

147

finally discovered, will prove our conceptions of time to be illusory. By attempting to raise a superstructure upon a basis of false premises we have merely added mystery to mystery.

Scientists, doctors and philosophers have recognized the reality of the phenomenon. Einstein, with his theory of relativity, showed the world that people had got their ideas of time entirely wrong. Even J.W. Dunne, in *An Experiment with Time*, proved the existence of precognition, and the absurdity of our old-fashioned conception of time as a single dimension.

I find it instructive to look again at Dunne's precise words to me when we discussed this at Broughton Castle. He had described to me the various kinds of time, and illustrated vividly the fallacy behind our common conceptions of it:

> Time must have a time in which to move, and that time must have yet another time in which to move – and so on ... imagine your life to be like a knife. You are walking along the edge of the knife. One end is your birth, the other your death. You move along this knife, watching your step lest you fall off or slide along it too quickly.
>
> It is only when you reach the end, when you die, that you awaken to the fact that the knife itself is moving, upwards and onwards, sweeping every atom of human experience, emotion and substance with it. You will die, but your consciousness goes on in this unsuspected tide, finding itself in a four-dimensional world ... in Time 2 one will be able to go backwards and forwards along the dimension of time at will.

By 'Time 2' Dunne was speaking of the *other* dimension of time, in which time, as we conceive it, moves.

At this point I asked Dunne: 'You mean I will be able to live in any period I like as the fancy takes me, choose my experiences and meet whom I like?'

To which Dunne replied: 'Exactly. I strongly suspect that as one passes from one stage to another one will come nearer to the truth of the thing – which I think will prove to be the Deity. The fact that there is time underlying time is really very comforting, and accounts now for the apparent cruelty of nature in creating beautiful things only to destroy them. I am convinced that nothing is ever lost.'

It will be seen that my interest in precognition is of long standing. Although not everyone goes along with Dunne's thinking today, there are plenty of scientists who acknowledge the reality of precognition and advance theories about it. Even Professor John Taylor of King's College, London, who tested Uri Geller, the psychic whose fork-bending exploits received wide publicity in the sixties, had gone some way to acknowledging the possibility of precognition, a phenomenon which he once discounted. His hypothesis is that perhaps the brain emits 'tachyons' – impulses travelling faster than light, thereby reaching into the future and then being reflected back to the brain, giving a person foreknowledge. The existence of these particles of energy which he has chosen to label 'tachyons' remains to be proved, of course.

Dr Stanley Krippner, Director of the Dream Laboratory at the Maimonides Medical Centre, New York, tells me that he is repeatedly experiencing what seems to be precognition in his own life. The examples are not always dramatic, but curious nevertheless. One night he had a dream about Vincent Price, the actor; tearing a piece of paper at random the following day, to retain information about current theatrical shows, he found a picture of the actor on the other side.

He dreamed about being at a party with the actress Joan Blondell, only to find, on switching on his radio the following morning, that she was being interviewed.

Dr Montagu Ullman, of the Department of Psychiatry, Maimonides Medical Centre, who has for years worked with Dr Krippner in the Dream Laboratory, told me recently of a curious premonition involving his colleague. 'I dreamed about Dr Krippner, and noticed something wrong with his mouth. The next day, while travelling in an unfamiliar section of New York, I saw a man coming towards me who, because of his very similar (and characteristic) way of walking, I thought might be Stanley [Krippner]. As he came closer I realized that he wasn't, but I was shocked to notice that he had a large red mass around his mouth, most likely a malignancy. That was a horror!'

Professor Emilio Servadio, President of the Rome Psychoanalytic Centre, and one of the world's leading psychoanalysts, tells me that he has frequently encountered the phenomenon of precognition in the course of his practice and researches. One astonishing incident happened many years ago, when one of Dr Servadio's patients described (for the purposes of analysis) a dream he had experienced; he had seen Dr Servadio's wife in a house near the sea, with some pretty children. Yet this patient had no reason at all to suppose that Mrs Servadio had, in fact, gone for a change to a little house near the sea, together with their small daughter and two little nieces, exactly as pictured in his dream.

Dr Servadio recalls how a lady doctor, Dr Fulvia Pontani Mayer, who was undergoing training in analysis with him experienced three precognitive dreams. 'On one occasion,' Dr Servadio told me, 'she dreamt of a baby elephant which she found very lovely and very clumsy. A few days after the dream, while walking in the Villa Borghese, she saw a baby elephant with its guardians, on their way to the zoo. This was a practically unique occurrence. In all my life I never heard of a baby elephant walking through the Villa Borghese except on the former occasion, and I think it will never happen to me again!'

Doctor Mayer had another dream in which a woman had a little monkey in her arms – only to come across the exact replica of her dream in a photograph in a magazine. On another occasion she had a 'preview' in a dream of a scene in which she visited a poor family, in her capacity of paediatrician. She had dreamed of being in the bedroom of a poor family, a little girl lying in bed between the husband and wife. The scene was exactly enacted later.

An idea for an anti-gravity machine came to Edwin Richman of Colchester, Essex, in a dream impressing him enough not only to draw it when he woke, but to take out a patent on it. Although Professor Eric Laithwaite, of Imperial College in London felt it was impracticable exactly as drawn, he tried it out with minor variations and constructed a machine which he believes will defy gravity. Why Mr Richman, who is not a scientist, should have had such a clear vision of such an unusual nature and application is simply a mystery.

The prevision of Dr Immanuel Velikovsky – then aged eighty-two and living in Princeton, New Jersey – enabled him to describe, with prophetic accuracy, what conditions would be like on the planet Venus. He described Venus as 'exceedingly hot', somewhere near 600 degrees Fahrenheit, in his book, *Worlds in Collision*, published over thirty-five years ago. Seventeen years later the Soviet space probe Venus 4 established that the temperature of Venus was 536° whereas when Velikovsky wrote his book scientists laughed at him. Velikovsky had further declared that Venus was a 'young' planet and still in process of formation, and not, as scientists insisted, an old and dead planet. Later research has proved him correct in this, too.

All over the world cases of apparent precognition are reported. As a phenomenon precognition manifests itself as consistently, if not to the same extent, as reports of ghosts and hauntings.

I have for long looked for some common factor in the numerous reports that have reached me. First, as to sex. Experiences do not appear to be equally divided. Women seem more prone to such experiences than men. Age does not seem to be in any way a factor; children as well as adults of every age have glimpsed the future. Health? Only a superficial observation is permissible here, since people are not necessarily objective about the state of their mental and physical health, and a detailed examination of the health records of every informant would entail more time and money than a lone researcher could afford. Perhaps such a project may be undertaken one day. For the moment, I can say that, going by the usual and normal criteria of intelligence, lucidity of expression, character as revealed by handwriting, and other factors, most of my informants would be considered normal. Few had any record of impaired faculties, or judgement inhibited or warped by trauma or mental ill-health.

Geographic considerations do not appear to affect the

capacity for experiencing precognition. People living alone, people living together in numbers, or families; those living in quiet, remote villages and others in crowded, noisy cities – all have come to experience foreknowledge.

If we can draw no statistical clues as to the nature of precognition or the circumstances in which it is most likely to be manifested, can we draw any conclusions as to the causes underlying it?

Professor Taylor's hypothesis about 'tachyons' – faster-than-light particles emitted by the brain, voyaging into and perceiving the future, and returning to record it, is to some degree anticipated by those who marvelled at the nature of human cells. It could be argued that to some degree at least cells have some type of built-in intelligence. There are billions of them in the human body, and the immense network of nerve cells in particular may constitute some mysterious transmitting and receiving system. If some form of energy is transmitted from the human body capable of travelling faster than light, it might not emanate from the brain itself. Nor, having travelled faster than light, and so into the future, would the impressions and messages necessarily be received directly by the brain? The brain might pick up the impulses after the outgoing energy waves had been reflected back, radar fashion, to the bodily source of transmission.

Is some type of mystical bent, or esoteric training and discipline, of help in foreseeing the future? There are innumerable cults and religions that claim that this is so, but there is nothing in my own records to suggest that ordinary people (as distinct from mystics, recluses, eccentrics, occultists and so on) are less prone to experience precognition; they seem, indeed, to be drawn from a cross-section of ages, educational levels, and social backgrounds.

An analysis of the questionnaires which were sent out to correspondents who responded to my appeal on Granada Television, however, shows a preponderance of females in proportion of two to one. So perhaps the widely held belief that women are more intuitive than men may have some basis in fact. An analysis of informants by ages revealed the average age of female and male informants as almost identical – fifty for women and forty-nine for men, although of course, the actual ages of those who had had such experiences varied very widely indeed – from a twelve-year-old schoolboy to a retired colonial civil servant of eighty-five. I am referring however to the ages of informants, not the age at which experiences were actually encountered; here there seems no discernible criterion of any sort.

Surprisingly few – a negligible proportion in fact – belonged to any society or group concerned with psychical research or organizations concerned with the arcane or occult. In other words, the experiences recorded happened to people neither consciously nor subconsciously predisposed to such things.

By far the largest numbers of cases of precognition concern dreams, and among corroborated accounts several concern drowning. Further, most such dreams presage accidents and disasters of one kind or another. Accidents or tragedies involving individuals are usually foreseen by friends or relatives, while larger-scale tragedies such as shipwrecks, train crashes, aviation disasters and natural misfortunes such as floods, earthquakes and hurricanes seem, for the most part, to occur to people unconnected with the places or the people subsequently involved.

This suggests to me that some psychic link may exist between people who hold each other in mutual friendship or affection, a factor which emerges also from an examination of accounts of telepathy.

Even a human concern for another person, perhaps not so strong as affection or even friendship, may establish a psychic link of some kind as yet undefined. An example could be that of John Buckmaster, of Chingford, whose vivid 'waking dream' (see earlier) of a building on fire was followed by a fire at Claybury Hospital in which an *ex-client* of his died.

A very few people seem to have a special capacity for

precognition. The late J.W. Dunne was one, and in his books he lists a considerable number of personal precognitive experiences, some trivial, some dramatic, whereas many people go through life without a single such experience. Mrs Lorna Middleton, who logs her precognitive 'feelings' with me regularly, achieves many accurate predictions so far as forecasts of future happenings are concerned, although they sometimes pre-empt something that happens the same evening, and within uncomfortable proximity of myself!

The details of places and buildings, first visualized in a kind of day-dream, or literally dreamed about beforehand, are often uncannily accurate, such as Mrs Goodsell's prevision of what her future home would look like, or Mrs Eisnor's certainty that a hurricane would devastate her farm. Such *déjà vu* is a form of precognition.

Yet after years of research into this problem, I have to ask myself how an effect can possibly precede a cause. The answer, I think, is that a future *must* exist; although the end-product of a complicated pattern of simultaneous happenings and interrelationships cannot be seen at the time, *one* result, out of perhaps hundreds of thousands of seemingly possible results will come to pass. In this sense, perhaps, there is a degree of predetermination.

If such a pattern of predetermination can be accepted as existing, messages of a future event may be transmitted backwards to the present – whether by means of faster-than-light 'tachyons' emitted from the brain of a human, travelling forwards into the future and returning with information, or by some method other than that postulated by Professor John Taylor. I do not know.

Some conclusion can be drawn, however, as to the physical conditions conducing to precognition. In most instances the 'mental gaze' or dreams come when the person is relaxed and free from the demands and distractions of daily life. It would seem that on some subliminal level, dormant capacities awaken and become operative. One can hardly go beyond that at the moment, for despite an immense amount of brain research which is in progress in many countries, nobody can *see* the effects of a brain working. One can merely see some evidence of brain activity by means of electrodes adhering to the person's head, or gold wire probes inserted with infinite care into the brain itself through a minuscule hole, so that impulses can be registered and recorded by complicated electronic apparatus. Yet the electrodes record impulses and changes in the thought-stream; the probes can be made to activate a particular part of the brain (in some instances, re-evoking to the person the symphonic strains of some long-forgotten concert). But that is not to see the brain at work or observe the interrelationship of its billions of cells. Still less does it tell us anything about 'mind' or the 'psyche'.

I can give no certain answer as to why and how precognition occurs. Nor has any scientist come up with the solution, either.

# 14   What is 'Time'?

Our human destinies seem to have one common basis –
time. For each of us, what we describe as time begins
when we are born, and ends at death. I have said this is
true of *human* destiny. Whether we have consciousness of
time in previous existences, as the believers in reincar-
nation maintain, or some part of our consciousness or
personality survives bodily death, as so many religious
and faiths postulate, is another matter.

Precognition, in the sense in which we have been
considering it, implies a human consciousness and is
something experienced during a human lifetime.

The phenomenon I have been dealing with is
foreknowledge – when the brain has been able to skip
*ahead of time*. Can we define, satisfactorily, the 'time' on
which so much is based? What do we think time is, and
are we right in what we think? Both precognition and
retrocognition imply that our conceptions of time are
either fallacious or woefully incomplete, or both.

Precognition, to be intelligible, demands an answer to
three unanswerable problems: the nature of time; the
actual cause of precognition; and the problem of free-will.

As to the nature of 'time', it is for most a subjective
thing. We think of time beginning with our birth, of
something called the 'present' moving constantly towards
the end of the journey – death.

That is our knowledge of what we choose to call time,
dictated by our own consciousness and senses, and within
our admitted mental limitations.

We all know that cannot entirely be the answer. We
were born of others – they had their time before we began

to experience ours. Our children will be experiencing time, both while we are alive and after we are dead. Is the butterfly, which lives for a day, conscious of time? Or the aphis fly, or the mole, or the tortoise that lives for over a century? We do not know, but I doubt if they look nostalgically back to youth, or fearfully forward to death. Most living things have an internal 'clock' which dictates a rhythm of living, and usually this inner timing relates to night and day and to the recurring seasons.

But we think of time as a *dimension*, which implies a beginning and an end. The fallacy of this is at once apparent when one applies the most elementary logic. Merely ask yourself, when did the universe start? If time had a beginning, then presumably before the universe started there was nothing. Where did all the something come from? If you could, in fact, enter a Time Machine à la H.G. Wells, how far back would you have to go to this alleged 'beginning'? Theologians have an easy answer, but there is a difference between dogma and reason, even though certain truths may remain forever elusive.

Our time measurement is based on the earth's rotation on its axis in its orbit around the sun. Some such measurement is necessary for the organization of our lives and our work. But in fact, convenient though our system is, the comparison of any moving object against a stationary object, or of two moving objects, or the period enacted by any particular kind of happening, would serve as well.

But, as Dr Alexis Carrell points out in *Man the Unknown*:

> For concrete man, time is very different from space. But the four dimensions would seem identical to an abstract man inhabiting the sidereal spaces. Although distinct from space, time is inseparable from it ... in nature, time is always found united to space. It is a necessary aspect of material beings. No concrete thing has only three spatial dimensions. A rock, a tree, and animal, cannot be instantaneous. Indeed, we are capable of building up in our minds beings entirely described within three dimensions. But all concrete things have four. And man extends both in time and space. *To an observer living far more*

*slowly than we do, he would appear as something narrow and
elongated, analogous to the incandescent trail of a meteor.*

This is a profound and important observation. Let us try
and imagine this timeless observer. A tree in Hyde Park
seems to burgeon as a sapling from the ground, rise, twist,
throw out branches, become festooned with leaves, wilt,
fade, fall, and do so repetitively with the seasons that
come and go, until the aged trunk withers and decays.
Every flower similarly, like a speeded-up cinematographic
film that compresses months into minutes, sprouts, twists,
turns, adapts, blooms – and dies. Areas of the world which
at one time shone green with grass, then turn brackish as
cities develop and buildings appear, then perhaps the
earth, where the cities once stood, now discoloured by the
ruins of war, reverts to desolation and stillness. The
merest spark of light betokens a volcanic eruption lasting
in human terms for days, spreading destruction and
despair over a huge area.

But the man whom Alexis Carrell says is extended in
both time and space 'possesses another aspect, impossible
to define clearly':

> For he is not wholly comprised within the physical
> continuum. Thought is not confined within time and space
> ... moreover, we know that clairvoyants may detect
> hidden things at great distances. Some of them perceive
> events which have already happened *or which will take place
> in the future. It should be noted that they apprehend the future in
> the same way as the past.*
>
> The time we observe in nature has no separate existence
> ... we ourselves create mathematical time. It is a mental
> construct, *an abstraction* indispensable to the building up of
> science.

This abstraction, as I pointed out in my introductory
chapter, leads us into false premises. But do not be
discouraged if, as a consequence, the underlying factors
which make precognition possible defy definition;
scientists and physicists, indeed philosophers too, are not
much better off so far as explanations go, even though
they may enjoy their quest.

The limitations of our minds make us think of time as a railway track. We get in at one station (birth), the changing scenes suggest to us the movement of what we call time, and then the buffer of our final station (death) come into view.

One school of thought believes that all the events of a lifetime coexist, past, present and future being one and a whole, of which the consciousness is not wholly aware. Of course, if the future already exists, if one's path is neatly tracked, a glimpse of the future becomes more intelligible. However, the inevitable inference arising from such a postulate makes no sense at all. If the future is ordained, why trouble to make decisions? Why assert yourself? Why bother with conflict, conscience, obligations, duties, development? Why swim against the all-powerful tide? In short, what happens to free-will, the conscious choice most of us try to assert, the dignity of individuality, of feeling that we have *our* hands on the steering-wheel and drive where we please?

The second supposition, that what has happened is still real and irreversible, and constitutes the past, while the future remains a complete blank, seems superficially logical until one remembers that, if this were so, precognition could never occur. How can you have cognizance of something that doesn't exist? There is cause and there is effect, presumably (though not necessarily, as precognition proves) in that order. You bang a drum, and a sound ensues. You throw a stone, and it goes through a window. But could you hear the throb of the drum *before* it is banged, and see the smashed window *before* the stone is thrown?

Then there would seem to be a third, if ambivalent and even confusing, alternative: the 'plastic future'. The past has happened, so far as *you* are concerned. For millions of others, millions of different 'pasts' have been experienced. All the time change is occurring in the lives of every inhabitant of this planet. The combination of their experiences forms a collective past (whether a collective consciousness, as Jung believed, is another matter). Likewise, is there a collective future – a combination of all that will transpire to each person, their destinies interreacting one upon another? Or amidst this unimaginable perpetuation of differing destinies, is there a separate destiny for every one – but one which each can alter, by each initial initiative, should they so wish?

This last concept does not rule out entirely precognition as a phenomenon. At any point in that continuous series of changes which we call 'time' a person may, perhaps, see clearly the future as it is likely to unfold. That future is correct as thing are, *then*. But, forewarned, the individual may reshape the future as it is when he sees it – hence the phrase 'plastic' future.

This last concept retrieves some measure of free-will, and acknowledges in a manner more acceptable to the human ego the individuality of man and his freedom to assert courage, judgement, spontaneity or even caprice in the pursuit of his personal destiny. It also acknowledges that precognitive glimpses of the future can and do occur.

The weak point in this last theory is that it is rare for one particular decision to affect the future. Certainly if, as has happened, a passenger refuses to board a plane because he is certain it will crash, he alters his particular future. Had he not heeded his precognition he would have died, but it has been beyond him to alter all the other factors affecting the disaster – the fatigue of the pilot through over-work, or a faulty altimeter, or unusual weather conditions which arise from innumerable different factors, or a bomb planted by a terrorist. He has altered *his* future, but the future in general he has not altered. The tragedy has merely one observer less. This is a problem which J.W. Dunne descibes as 'the classical objection to the notion of prophecy'.

Here, of course, we come back to Dunne's once sensational and (nowadays) less acceptable conundrum: that the 'present' if it moves in time at all, as we assume it does, must take time to do so. Therefore, says Dunne, there must be another 'time' in which Time 1 moves. But if Time 1 moves in Time 2 it must also take time to do so – there must be a third 'time'.

It is long ago that I interviewed J.W. Dunne on his

theories, and it is no easier to summarize his ideas now than it was then. A full exposition of the scientific justification adduced by Dunne in support of his extraordinary ideas may be read in full by anyone who choose. Just as Sigmund Freud may well be mistaken in ascribing so primary a role to sex in human psychology, yet he alerted the world to the fact that it was a different, and more vital, problem than had been supposed, so Dunne made the world think again about the nature of time: and focused attention on precognition as a factor of life.

Professor C.D. Broad has declared that he finds Dunne's endless series of times an untenable proposition. H.F. Saltmarsh, of the Society for Psychical Research, in his brief but succinct book on precognition published in 1938 (*Foreknowledge*, G. Bell & Sons, London) rejected Dunne's theories, but found Professor Broad's comprise idea of two-dimensional time logical, and a possible explanation of precognition of which, at the time Saltmarsh wrote his book, there were already nearly 250 cases in the files of the Society. The idea of 'two-dimensional time' is one in which it is not conceived as being, so to speak, a straight path between north and south, but extending from east to west also.

Now we are dealing with a phenomenon which we consider other than normal. We have elected to call precognition *paranormal,* that being the fashionable and acceptable word in present use. Most words are symbols, being emotive and not merely conveying facts. They were devised by human beings, who have emotions and their suggestibility is often conveyed to others without the user of the word being aware of it. It behoves us to look critically, even suspiciously, at the word 'normal' when considering the whole range of subjects that are imperfectly understood. Are we not loading the dice? Are we not presupposing that what we know, and think we understand, is normal, and that all beyond the range of our present knowledge, all that defies scientific explanation, is 'paranormal', 'abnormal' and so on? If so, we are the victims of our own vanity and presumed logic. We are assuming too readily that our perceptions are accurate and acceptable; that we have the same degree of perception; that the consciousness is merely the opposite of unconsciousness, and that our consciousness operates at an even-level efficiency, or is as acute in one situation as in another.

F.W.H. Myers, one of the founders of the Society for Psychical Research, and co-author with two other founders, Edmund Gurney and Frank Podmore of that masterly, if forbidding, compendium of the unusual or unbelievable, *Phantasms of the Living*, (Kegan Paul, 1918) the world as early as 1886 that human consciousness was no more than the tip of the iceberg.

Myers was right. There are many levels of consciousness, which he chose to describe as the 'subliminal'. Whether he was correct in his belief that, on these lower levels of consciousness, each human being was in touch with all the others, in a merging of millions of different consciousnesses, must remain a matter for proof, although telepathy and the appearance of phantoms of the living, often far away from the place where the living person happens to be, adds colour to his hypothesis. Myers asked: 'Is there any convincing evidence that geniuses, for example, are also endowed with precognitive, telepathic and clairvoyant gifts?'

Here again the answer to Myers is surely 'yes'. Typical was the experience of the German poet, Goethe (1749-1832):

One rainy summer's evening, Goethe was strolling through the woods with a friend, when he was astounded to see, walking ahead, another acquaintance clad in dressing-gown and slippers. Such unsuitable clothing in wet weather suggested the man had taken leave of his senses; at the very least, he would catch a chill, and Goethe spoke to him to this effect. But there was no answer. However, when Goethe got home, he found the wanderer, in dressing-gown and slippers, sitting by the fireside. He explained that he had been caught in a shower on his way to visit Goethe and had borrowed his first available change of clothing to dry himself off while he waited for Goethe's return.

The explanation relieved Goethe, but did nothing to explain why he should have seen his friend in the woods.

Socrates (469-399BC) had a highly-developed sense of precognition. Once, out on a stroll with a group of friends, he elected to take a quite different, and unaccountable, course from the rest, and urged his friends to follow him. Most of them saw no reason to follow him on this changed route and went their chosen way. Those who ignored his advice were seriously injured by a rampaging herd of wild boars.

Once Socrates turned to a friend and told him not to proceed with a secret project he had in mind. The friend looked curiously at Socrates, for he had neither hinted at nor confided his secret project. Socrates' friend was in fact planning an assassination, but had at that stage told no one, nor were there circumstances, or a past record of behaviour, from which such an inference could be drawn. The friend, regrettably, ignored the advice, proceeded with his plans, carried out the assassination, and was in due course arrested, tried and executed.

Did Goethe see what he thought he saw? Did Socrates harbour, perhaps unknown in his subconscious mind, suspicions as to the character of his friend, suspicions that had built up to a picture of him planning something desperate and dangerous? Did Goethe wonder (again, on a deeper level of consciousness), why he had not seen his friend lately, and consider that if his friend did choose such a day to call, he would surely get wet and need to dry off? And, if such thoughts percolated into his *conscious* mind, were they, by some fault in the synapses or valves that keep the traffic of light-waves moving back from the eye to the cerebral cortex, transmit them *forward* from the brain to the eye? If so, Goethe could have seen a vision, which by a reflex action would thereupon be transmitted backwards, from the eye to the brain, making the whole thing unnervingly real to him.

Obviously we cannot answer these questions. Goethe and Socrates are only two of a large number of people who could rightfully be called geniuses, who had precognitive experiences, but my own researches, and those of others in this field, do not suggest that such experiences are more common with the intelligent or super-intelligent than with the average.

In his seventeenth Myers Memorial Lecture to the Society for Psychical Research, Sir Cyril Burt, Professor of Psychology Emeritas at London University, related how Einstein asked J. Piaget, an expert on child psychology, what a child's understanding of time was? Einstein:

> asked him if he would attempt an investigation to determine whether the young child's understanding of time arose from his prior understanding of variations in distance and speed, or whether his notion of time was primary. Briefly, it may be said, Piaget's results indicated that the small child is a little relativist rather than a little absolutist ... As both Stern [L.W. Stern] and Valentine [C.A. Valentine] have noted, the child talks about the future long before he talks about the past. Indeed, as Valentine observes, 'his wish-fulfilments are often expressed as though they were actual precognition'. He relates how his little daughter observed 'Tomorrow I had such a big helping of Christmas pudding'. Her mother explained that it was still the day before Christmas. But next afternoon the child replied: 'It wasn't the day before. I told you I did have a big helping tomorrow'.

Thomas Carter, a Liverpool inventor and designer, has evolved a short and simple theory of his own to account for precognition. He takes as his starting-point Newton's third law of motion, pointing out that to every action there is an equal and opposite reaction, and illustrates his point in this graphically simple way:

> Stand on a banana skin. You go one way, the banana skin the other. A child stands on the edge of a trolley and then jumps off – the child goes one way, the trolley the other; or when a bullet is fired from a gun, the bullet goes one way, the gun the other, and kicks you in the shoulder.
>
> To every action (which is the explosion propelling the bullet) there is an equal and opposite reaction, which is the explosion propelling the gun into one's shoulder.

Now take Newton's third law one step further. Consider your life-line similar to the barrel of a gun. Instead of a chemical explosion to propel a bullet we experience a mental explosion (shock) and the lines of force that it creates travel along the lifeline in equal and opposite directions.

The force moving along the life-line into the future we know as memory, the equal and opposite lines of force into the past I know now as precognition, so that the you that is in the past to the event will receive a vision or a hunch of what will happen.

Mr Carter believes that the strength or force of an emotional event (the sort, if you like, that leaves a mark of trauma) must cast its shadow before. This is the inescapable inference of the development of his theory, as he puts it:

> As time passes into the future, memory about an emotional event fades as the force carrying it becomes weaker, so this means that an event that made you remember vividly after it happened then fades; will also have been in your mind slightly up to a week before the event and then for the last week quite vivid if you can find it.

When one remembers an incident from one's past, that one thought had faded, it is usually due to some occurrence in the present being similar to when the incident happened. For a second, you see through your eyes of the past. This sudden vision of the past gives your memory of the incident an extra boost, and in this instance your memory of what happened is more vivid than it should have been so long after the incident took place. This means that memory could be longer than precognition: but the reason is not the mental explosion in the past, but the slight explosion that occurred when you remembered afresh.

He also believes that we are equipped to sense and prepare for crises and emotional shocks of particular strength:

If in your life something so big happens to you that you never forget it, and it is always in your conscious mind, *then you will find that this affects your life very greatly prior to the event*. Possibly from the minute you are born it will, in fact, shape your character considerably. Your mind, in fact tries to adapt you to cope with or avoid these problems from the possible future before you actually reach them.

In a previous work, *Mysterious Worlds* (W.H. Allen, 1970), I dealt with a range of psychic phenomena, including to some extent precognition and what are commonly called 'out-of-the-body' experiences. I have many instances of these (mostly unpublished, and this is not the place to adduce them). But A.B. Campbell, a land surveyor, living in Berkshire since he retired from the colonial service, has some telling observations to make on the subject of precognition. I must confess that until he pointed it out, I had not thought of any connection between these so-called 'out-of-the-body' experiences, sometimes called 'astral projection' and precognition. But, just as telepathy and hallucinations, or telepathy and precognition, are often related, so the phenomena of astral projection and precognition can be related, or merge:

> You will appreciate from your own investigations that in psychical research, the phenomena of telepathy, for instance, is outside SPACE and TIME. Then again, in some miraculous healings the TIME element has disappeared, for cures are instantaneous and permanent. And although the experiences of the Yogi and other mystics are subjective, and not shared by others, one and all tell us 'there is no yesterday or tomorrow, there is only a present NOW'. [Refer Eckhart in sermon XC, 'The Interpretation of Mystic and Cosmic Experiences' by Dr Robert Crookall. p.76.]
>
> The fusion of SPACE with TIME is what the physical scientist has termed 'SPACE-TIME'. The theory of 'SPACE-TIME' originated with the Russian scientist, Minkowski, and in the hands of another Russian scientist, P.D. Ouspensky, the connection between 'SPACE-TIME' and the 'MYSTIC' state or continuum was emphasized. He lays stress on the limitations of the human intellect, which follows alike from the mystical and the mathematical

implications of 'SPACE-TIME'. In other words, there is a limit to human thought, because the implications of 'SPACE-TIME' are only imperfectly understood. Nevertheless, human beings are simultaneously inhabitants of the world of space and time and the continuum of 'SPACE-TIME'.

At this point in his theorizing, Mr Campbell goes on to draw a connection between 'astral projection' and 'precognition':

> This dual existence is evident when the MIND – the seat of consciousness – 'floats' into 'SPACE-TIME', as it does during sleep, or when the patient on the operating table is under the influence of an anaesthetic. In most cases, the subject may remain oblivious to both worlds, or have dreams which are distorted and nonsensical and forgotten on waking. On the other hand these 'out-of-the-body' experiences (for that is what they are) now and then do penetrate the realm of reality (SPACE-TIME) and register true pictures of people or of events which have occurred *or will occur later*. You have recorded some of these which took place and proved real when the dreamers awoke.

Like most people interested in precognition, Mr Campbell has followed the theories of J.W. Dunne. In his case, studying Dunne has led him to conclusions of his own, in many respects parallel to mine:

> Dunne holds that in dreams (and perhaps in other states) it is possible to survey the future as one surveys a plain from a hill. Now this is exactly the conclusion come to by the mathematician Minkowski in dealing with the primary 'SPACE-TIME' equation. He noticed that SPACE and TIME enter the equation in precisely the same manner, and that therefore SPACE and TIME must be equivalent to each other. He concluded that TIME is a SPACE dimension which is imperfectly understood by our minds.
>
> Needless to say I was greatly interested to read what Minkowski had discovered mathematically, because some

years ago I tried to visualize this 'puzzle' of SPACE-TIME by means of a diagram and here it is.

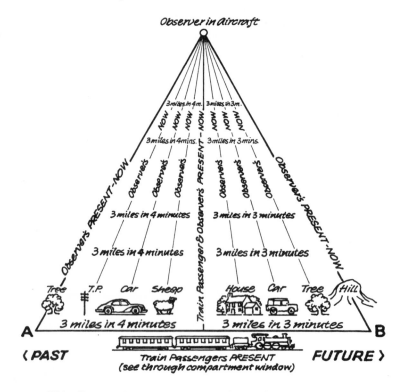

This diagram is an attempt to indicate that a man sitting in the compartment of a railway carriage merely sees 'through a glass, darkly' his passing PRESENT. From this position he cannot see his PAST. Neither is his FUTURE known to him. But the observer at 'O' in the aircraft sees the passenger's past, present and FUTURE as one NOW for from his altitude SPACE and TIME have fused into one, namely SPACE-TIME.

NOTE: the six miles distance (Space) and the seven minutes (Time) taken to cover that distance have disappeared altogether at 'O' (the Observer's position in the aircraft). SPACE and TIME have fused into one present – NOW, the SPACE-TIME of the mystic and the physical scientist. The Observer in the aircraft sees the two trees, the telephone pole, the two cars, the sheep, the house and the hill at one glance, INSTANTANEOUSLY. He sees also the passenger's past, present and future in this diagram as one present – NOW.

I think that J.W. Dunne, who once explained his theories to me with such patience and clarity, would heartily have approved of Mr Campbell's efforts to carry the banner, and to express a theory of precognition in a simple and understandable manner – no easy thing with a subject embodying so many different, related and complex sciences. In stressing the limitations of the human intellect when considering space-time, Mr Campbell is certainly right. Few people can conceive anything in other than three dimensions, and those who try to do otherwise find themselves in a metaphysical maze. He summarizes his conclusions thus:

> Taking another glance at this diagram, we notice that at 'O' (the Observer's position in the aircraft) TIME is one with SPACE, as Minkowski has shown and, this being so, it is indistinguishable from SPACE. This means that TIME has no beginning because a beginning implies a 'past' (which is 'space' which disappears in SPACE-TIME). On this showing, 'time' can have no end either (eternity?) All very confusing to our three-dimensional thinking.
>
> In precognition we are confronted with the 'effect' before the 'cause', indicating that the mind can be as independent of TIME and it can be of SPACE. But 'cause' and 'effect' cannot exist *apart* from 'SPACE' *and* 'TIME', because space and time do not exist as independent entities.

He concludes, I think correctly, with the observation that 'our conception of time forms one of the major difficulties in understanding it. One doubts whether we shall ever understand it. Our conception of TIME is due to a structure of our minds which can deal only with a three-dimensional world. SPACE-TIME is a continuum of four dimensions which is difficult to imagine'.

The unity of past, present and future which constitute what we call time is perhaps a key to the mystery of precognition. But it is clear that the nature of human personality, the nature of time and, indeed, our fallacious ideas on matter, by which we separate, in our arguments and deductive processes, the 'material' and the 'immaterial' obscure our quest for the truth. We must get used to the idea (a hard one to accept) that matter and energy are the same thing, that there is no true dividing line between living and non-living things. The chair you sit upon is not dead wood, but a whirling universe of energy, or energy disciplined in such a way as to seem solid and substantial. The carbon atoms that comprise it are, each of them, a universe in which electrons are whirling around their nucleus of protons and neutrons.

Einstein carried this relationship even further. At certain speeds, physical objects cease to be physical objects as we know them, but fields of electrical force or energy. Indeed it would seem by his reasoning that if an object could travel with the speed of light it would be transformed into light.

If, as with precognition, we are therefore bemused by time, it is not surprising, and nothing to feel depressed about. We happen to be upon the earth, but in other parts of the universe time means something different. Something happening in what we call 'the present' could be seen in different parts of the universe at totally different times, according to the distance of the vantage points of the different observers. For the time taken for light to travel to different parts of the universe could differ by hundreds of years. By the same token, time becomes nonsense when we look through a telescope. To us the time is *now*. And *now* we see Andromeda, two million light years away, Betelgeuse (one of the largest stars and thousands of times brighter than the sun) three hundred light years away. Thus, by what appears an absurdity, what happened two million years ago, and what happened three hundred years ago, appear to us *at the same moment*. For what we see has travelled towards us with the speed of light, and has taken those differing periods to do so.

In short, the further you look out into space, the farther you travel back in time. Looking up at the sky on a cloudless night, you see simultaneously thousands of different pasts at once. If time plays surprising tricks with us, it is not so surprising, for the universe, and the space-time which is an inherent part of it, is full of surprises. I can do no better than finish on this quote from *Psychology and Psychical Research*, by Sir Cyril Burt. It is one of the finest, most carefully considered, knowledgeable and most clearly expounded papers ever to be delivered on the subject:

> Sir Alistair Hardy has done well to remind us that no sharp line can be drawn between the pronouncements of mediums and the pronouncement of the mystics. To this I would like to add that a too exclusive attention has in the past been paid to the writings of the more celebrated mystics, whether in the field of religion, poetry, philosophy, or nature; we ought also to collect and analyse reports from numerous men and women in humbler walks of life who have had very similar experiences. In my own enquiries, in order to secure first-hand impressions uncontaminated by literary influences, I separated the more highly educated persona from the remainder. I found that even among the 'unsophisticated' the descriptions still agreed to a remarkable extent with each other and with the traditional reports. The fundamental feeling is the unreality of separateness. Space and time segregate both things and persons, and are therefore held to be unreal. *Nature, material things, the visible and the tangible, are merely fragmentary and somewhat confused appearances, half revealing, half concealing, a unified whole. Spatial size and spatial distance lose their importance: we may recall Ramsey's remark – 'Stars may be huge, but they cannot think and love.'*

Time means no more than an opportunity for things to change and for persons to strive – the possibility of progress and improvement. 'Reality' is experienced, not as something lasting or everlasting, but timeless.

# Index

172